W9-ABI-212

Fantasy

THE GREENHAVEN PRESS COMPANION TO
Literary Movements and Genres

Fantasy

Wendy Mass, *Book Editor*
Stuart P. Levine, *Book Editor*

Daniel Leone, *President*
Bonnie Szumski, *Publisher*
Scott Barbour, *Managing Editor*
David M. Haugen, *Series Editor*

Greenhaven Press, Inc., San Diego, CA

Library of Congress Cataloging-in-Publication Data

Fantasy / Wendy Mass and Stuart P. Levine, book editors.
        p. cm. — (Literary movements and genres)
     Includes bibliographical references and index.
      ISBN 0-7377-1085-3 (pbk. : alk. paper) —
    ISBN 0-7377-1086-1 (lib. bdg. : alk. paper)
      1. Fantasy literature, English—History and criticism.
    2. Fantasy literature, American—History and criticism.
    3. Fantasy literature—History and criticism—Theory, etc.
    4. Fantasy literature—Appreciation. I. Mass, Wendy,
    1967– . II. Levine, Stuart P., 1968– . III. Series.

    PR149.F35 F37   2002
    823'.0876609—dc21   2001033276
                                                      CIP

Cover photo: A.K.G., Berlin/SuperStock

CONTENTS

Chapter 1: Understanding the Fantasy Genre

Chapter 2: Exploring Themes and Conventions

imaginary world by a sense of wonder that amazes both
the reader and the characters within the story.

Chapter 3: The State of the Genre Today

FOREWORD

The study of literature most often involves focusing on an individual work and uncovering its themes, stylistic conventions, and historical relevance. It is also enlightening to examine multiple works by a single author, identifying similarities and differences among texts and tracing the author's development as an artist.

While the study of individual works and authors is instructive, however, examining groups of authors who shared certain cultural or historical experiences adds a further richness to the study of literature. By focusing on literary movements and genres, readers gain a greater appreciation of influence of historical events and social circumstances on the development of particular literary forms and themes. For example, in the early twentieth century, rapid technological and industrial advances, mass urban migration, World War I, and other events contributed to the emergence of a movement known as American modernism. The dramatic social changes, and the uncertainty they created, were reflected in an increased use of free verse in poetry, the stream-of-consciousness technique in fiction, and a general sense of historical discontinuity and crisis of faith in most of the literature of the era. By focusing on these commonalities, readers attain a more comprehensive picture of the complex interplay of social, economic, political, aesthetic, and philosophical forces and ideas that create the tenor of any era. In the nineteenth-century American romanticism movement, for example, authors shared many ideas concerning the preeminence of the self-reliant individual, the infusion of nature with spiritual significance, and the potential of persons to achieve transcendence via communion with nature. However, despite their commonalities, American romantics often differed significantly in their thematic and stylistic approaches. Walt Whitman celebrated the communal nature of America's open democratic society, while Ralph Waldo

Emerson expressed the need for individuals to pursue their own fulfillment regardless of their fellow citizens. Herman Melville wrote novels in a largely naturalistic style whereas Nathaniel Hawthorne's novels were gothic and allegorical.

Another valuable reason to investigate literary movements and genres lies in their potential to clarify the process of literary evolution. By examining groups of authors, literary trends across time become evident. The reader learns, for instance, how English romanticism was transformed as it crossed the Atlantic to America. The poetry of Lord Byron, William Wordsworth, and John Keats celebrated the restorative potential of rural scenes. The American romantics, writing later in the century, shared their English counterparts' faith in nature; but American authors were more likely to present an ambiguous view of nature as a source of liberation as well as the dwelling place of personal demons. The whale in Melville's *Moby-Dick* and the forests in Hawthorne's novels and stories bear little resemblance to the benign pastoral scenes in Wordsworth's lyric poems.

Each volume in Greenhaven Press's Companions to Literary Movements and Genres series begins with an introductory essay that places the topic in a historical and literary context. The essays that follow are carefully chosen and edited for ease of comprehension. These essays are arranged into clearly defined chapters that are outlined in a concise annotated table of contents. Finally, a thorough chronology maps out crucial literary milestones of the movement or genre as well as significant social and historical events. Readers will benefit from the structure and coherence that these features lend to material that is often challenging. With Greenhaven's Literary Movements and Genres in hand, readers will be better able to comprehend and appreciate the major literary works and their impact on society.

INTRODUCTION: THE LITERATURE OF IMPOSSIBILITY

The term *fantasy literature* typically evokes images of fire-breathing dragons; wizards with tall, floppy hats; elves; gnomes; scantily clad maidens in distress and the armored knights who gallop in to save them. Although these are typical archetypes of the genre, there is much more to this diverse branch of fiction. With its roots in some of the oldest recorded texts from Egypt and Babylonia, and found in the works of Homer, Aristophanes, and even Shakespeare, fantasy literature has existed for many centuries and in many forms.

Perhaps the earliest form of fantasy is mythology. The basic characteristics of myth are much the same as those of fantasy literature. Myths attempt to delve into the realm of the impossible and offer up some rational explanation for that which cannot be explained. Similarly, modern fantasy literature offers the reader an impossible world or situation and then goes on to put parameters around it, making sense out of something that seems unreal. The significance of myth has been described as seeking to identify basic guideposts for human behavior and morality that can withstand the ever-changing whims of culture and society. In this same way, fantasy literature attempts to reexamine age-old questions of morality in the completely unfamiliar context of a whole new world.

Modern fantasy borrows many of the conventions of mythology, but the literary format stems from a much more recent period of human history. Although fantastic elements appear in many works of literature throughout the ages, the creation of a fantasy genre is most often traced to the nineteenth century. Lewis Carroll is often considered the "father" of modern fantasy literature because his most popular novels offered settings and characters that were both bizarre and yet somehow recognizable. *Alice's Adventures in Wonderland*

and *Through the Looking Glass* present a world that is irrational—or perhaps rational only unto itself—but not so much so that the reader cannot at least follow the odd pattern that runs through the story. However, in the late nineteenth century Carroll's work was considered best suited for children. Although adults could relish the satire in the looking-glass world, academics frowned upon the fantastic elements and emphasized the artistic superiority of more "realistic" fiction.

Although Lewis Carroll may have put fantasy literature on the literary map, it was not until almost a hundred years later that fantasy would establish itself as a serious genre. Released in the mid-1950s, J.R.R. Tolkien's *The Lord of the Rings* portrayed an epic struggle of a small race of people, called Hobbits, against a tyrannical source of great evil in their fantasy world of Middle Earth. Tolkien's books languished for nearly a decade before being catapulted into fame. During the social unrest of the 1960s, college students spent a lot of time looking at the reality that had been built for them. Choosing to reject this reality and the status quo on a number of different levels, an enormous number of young people jumped on Tolkien's fantasy bandwagon, finding within his texts relevant political messages about the strength of the underdog against oppression. College campuses were covered with copies of the books as well as students proudly participating in clubs, open readings, and wearing buttons that stated "Frodo Lives!" Tolkien's timeless saga, which had taken him more than twenty years to write, had become a phenomenon. From that day forward, the market for fantasy literature grew at an almost exponential rate.

Today this trend continues with best-selling works by authors such as Ursula K. Le Guin, Steven R. Donaldson, Robert Jordan, Piers Anthony, Terry Brooks, and Orson Scott Card. In the year 2000 the fantasy market saw a popular explosion that outshone even Tolkien's phenomenon. The release of the fourth book in British author J.K. Rowling's Harry Potter series, *Harry Potter and the Goblet of Fire,* saw a kind of success that was unparalleled not only in fantasy literature but also in the history of the printed word. The story of a young wizard learning to find his way in his fantasy environment captured the hearts of youngsters and adult readers alike. The initial printing of 3.8 million copies was sold out in less than a week. The book's U.S. publisher, Scholastic, attempted to meet the demand by immediately putting out another 3 million copies. With Harry Potter fan clubs, websites, games, clothing, merchandise, and even a big-budget Hollywood film, the phenomenon clearly demonstrates a need for fantasy in today's modernized world.

The current popularity of fantasy literature is evident. Most bookstores now have entire aisles dedicated to the genre, and promotions consistently keep them on displays at the front of the store. Some critics explain this recent surge in popularity as evidence of a backlash from the constraints of overly complicated lives. Myths attempted to place order where there was none. People have spent a lot of time in exactly this pursuit and have now reached a point where they are saddled under the yoke of an endless list of laws, rules, and regulations about how to survive in such a fast-paced world. Perhaps people are now looking back toward antiquity and fantasy to find, as one critic put it, "a clearer, simpler ethical guide than our stacks of legal code books."[1] With the help of a J.R.R. Tolkien or a J.K. Rowling every few decades, the genre of fantasy literature is guaranteed to remain in place as a steady guidepost.

NOTE

1. John H. Timmerman, *Other Worlds: The Fantasy Genre.* Bowling Green, OH: Bowling Green State University Popular Press, 1983, p. 23.

WHAT IS FANTASY?

To many people, fantasy literature is a mental passport to any place in the universe. Whether that place truly exists is of less importance than the fantastic journey and discoveries that await any who choose to enter the story. This particular literary genre has waxed and waned over the years. It has seen periods of popular success as well as entire centuries in which it was considered unfashionable or even a representation of ignorance. However, it has its roots in some of the oldest stories ever told, both orally and with the written word.

THE ORIGINS OF FANTASY

The concept of fantasy in literature has been around for a very long time. In fact, some of the earliest works of literature were precursors of what we would consider modern fantasy. As far back as 2000 B.C. the ancient Egyptians were putting down stories of the unreal on papyrus. One scroll recovered from that period contained a story called "The Tale of the Shipwrecked Sailor." It is the story of a young man who sets out to sea and is shipwrecked on an island where he encounters a genie (in the guise of a fifty-foot bearded snake). The genie torments the sailor while he struggles to stay alive and find a way off the island. Finally, after the sailor narrowly escapes the island with his life, the entire place disappears from sight and he returns home. "The Tale of the Shipwrecked Sailor" exhibits some of the archetypal elements of later myth or fantasy. It is the story of an uninitiated young hero who must battle and outwit forces much greater than himself in order to return home. The genie itself could even be viewed as the precursor to fantasy's most typical villain, the dragon.

A number of such examples of fantasy are found in ancient texts. From Babylonia came *The Epic of Gilgamesh*, an ancient tale that is still widely read today, of a powerful king and his bumbling companion who set out on great adventures and battled fire-breathing beasts. *Gilgamesh* and "The Ship-wrecked Sailor" are but two of many ancient tales that use fantastic, unreal settings to showcase the very human attributes of strength, intelligence, allegiance, and morality. Even the Old Testament, although primarily a religious text as opposed to literature, is full of references to stories involving magic and the supernatural. These stories, much like other forms of fantasy literature, are focused on humankind's struggle to come closer to an understanding of the infinite, undefinable, driving force of their world. These same desires to explore the uniquely human are recurring themes in fantasy literature and have persisted into the modern era.

DEFINING FANTASY

With all of the influences of myth, archaic adventure, and religious doctrine, it is not easy to define exactly what constitutes fantasy literature. Critics have argued over definitions for many years, claiming that some are too broad and others too narrow. Richard Matthews, author of *Fantasy: The Liberation of Imagination*, claims that "fantasy, as a distinct literary genre, . . . may best be thought of as a fiction that elicits wonder through elements of the supernatural or impossible. It consciously breaks free from mundane reality."[1] This narrowing, however, allows for genres like horror and utopian fiction to be classified as sub-genres of fantasy. This is acceptable to some, but to purists of horror fiction, for example, the secondary classification may be a point of contention.

The most common genre confusion, however, stems from the hazy boundary that exists between science fiction and fantasy. Science fiction often deals with modernized worlds with technological wonders while fantasy usually inhabits premodern realms. Still, the borders are never clear-cut and crossings occur, as in Piers Anthony's Apprentice Adept series, which revolves around two mirror-image worlds, one of which is ruled by magic and the other is ruled by technology. The general consensus among both critics and readers is that science fiction focuses on extraordinary occurrences and situations, based on theoretical projections of known scientific and natural laws. Fantasy, on the other hand, focuses on extraordinary occurrences that have little, if any, grounding in the physical laws of this world. Critic Eric Rabkin suggests that the genres are simply two ends of the same spectrum. Indeed, truly masterful fantasy paints a world that seems so real and so well detailed that it becomes easy to see the far-reaching connections that exist between the laws of this world and the imagined one.

CHOOSE YOUR FANTASY

Within the confines of the genre itself, there exist a number of general categories or classifications. By the very nature of the genre, much of fantasy literature cannot be pigeon-holed into one particular grouping. However, Susan Lehr, who penned the article "Fantasy: Inner Journeys for Today's Children," feels that there are some distinct categories into which most fantasy can be placed.

The first, High Fantasy, describes classic tales of knights, dragons, wizards, and magic. Lehr feels that J.R.R. Tolkien and C.S. Lewis were the ones responsible for defining this category. High Fantasy is typically set in a medieval world and often contains many of the archetypal images and myths associated with worldwide folk legend, such as elves, goblins, dragons, and wizards. With the creation of their now-classic realms of Middle Earth and Narnia, Tolkien and Lewis set the groundwork for many authors to come. Today this field probably makes up the largest percentage of fantasy work, including the notable works of authors such as Anthony, Le Guin, Brooks, Jordan, and many others.

Lehr's next category is Time Slip Fantasy. This includes works in which the action takes place in the reader's primary world, but in a different period in history. One of the most classic examples of this was Mark Twain's *A Connecticut Yankee in King Arthur's Court.* Originally published in 1889, the story involves the activities of a nineteenth century man suddenly flung back in time to Medieval England. There he must come to grips with life in ancient times and, at the same time, learn a little about himself. This vehicle of exploring the past through the eyes of a contemporary individual is sometimes used to help young people learn about history and social studies.

One such example given by Lehr is a book called *The Devil's Arithmetic.* It chronicles the events of a young Jewish girl who is suddenly thrown back in time to Nazi Germany where she slips into the life of a young girl named Chaya. As the book progresses, the modern girl begins to lose herself in the identity of Chaya and before long, the readers lose themselves as well. Both protagonist and reader begin to experience the events of Chaya's persecution nearly firsthand. Lehr feels that works such as these can be invaluable learning tools in the classroom. "They explore the reality of history firsthand and see the horror of battles, gas ovens, segregation, discrimination. Textbooks can never convey the personal response that a book like *The Devil's Arithmetic* emits."[2]

Another of Lehr's categories is Animal Fantasy. It is fairly common within the genre to encounter animals that talk and think, but this category deals with books that have such characters as the primary movers in the story. With its origins as far back as 600 B.C.E., this type of fantasy has been around since *Aesop's Fables* introduced us to a famous footrace between a tortoise and a hare. More recent installments include works such as George Orwell's *Animal Farm* and Richard Adams's *Watership Down*. In these stories, we see events unfold through the unusual perspective of an animal's eyes. The impossibility of these animals conversing, reading, writing, and even attempting political coups demands that such stories sit firmly on the shelves of fantasy literature. However, their unusual nature warrants a subcategory all its own.

Another very popular type of fantasy is sometimes referred to as Humorous Fantasy. Stories such as Roald Dahl's *Matilda* and *Charlie and the Chocolate Factory* are good examples of fantasy with a humorous and nearly absurd twist to them. Robert Asprin's *Myth* series, which focused on the comical misadventures of an apprentice magician and a homeless demon, was a large commercial success in the 1980s. Farcical adventures are often a great way to introduce young readers to the worlds of fantasy literature. Lehr believes that it

> pulls reluctant readers into wanting to become independent readers. Strong themes are couched in humorous adventures that kids relate to enthusiastically, and when done well . . . they make the reader laugh and clamor for more. You never convinced a child to become an active fluent reader by telling her that is was intrinsically good for her and that she would be a better person for the experience. Make a child laugh and enjoy the experience, however, and she'll be back for more.[3]

A great example of this philosophy in action is the success of J.K. Rowling's Harry Potter books. Many parents and critics credit these light and humorous books with reintroducing the joys of reading to a generation of children who don't often look beyond their video games and movies.

THE ELEMENTS OF FANTASY

Although fantasy may have many faces, they all have some common elements. For example, a fantasy is typically formulated around a journey or a quest. In addition, the story often takes place in another world—one that is distinct, yet somehow similar, to that of the reader. Typically, an element of magic is the basic foundation of a world that also contains strange places and odd creatures. Scholars and critics have studied fantasy writing and have found a number of common threads that run throughout all works in the genre.

A MYTHIC STORY

One of the most basic elements of a traditional fantasy is a story line. Homer's *The Odyssey*, for example, exhibits a classic story line common to fantasy literature. Odysseus, the hero of the tale, sets out on a journey to return home after the Trojan War. Along the way he is faced with a series of obstacles that he must overcome to eventually reach his goal—in this case, the reunion with his wife and son. The many adventures and setbacks en route to his homeland provide the compelling narrative that keeps the reader wondering if Odysseus will ever see his family again.

What is important about the narrative structure of *The Odyssey*—as well as most fantasy literature—is that it is based on myth. That is, the narrative is engaging in itself and can represent different things to different readers. In this way, fantasy story lines are unlike moralistic fairy tales. "The Little Boy Who Cried Wolf," for example, is an allegory, a story that has a simple and transparent message. There is little more to the story than the lesson it is clearly intended to teach. Mythic fantasy, on the other hand, tells a tale that can be more loosely interpreted. Although it still can attempt to set up certain guideposts for human behavior, fantasy is open to broader interpretations and multiple meanings. In fact, most fantasy authors will balk at having their work referred to as allegory. Ursula K. Le Guin goes so far as to say, "I hate allegories. A is 'really' B, and a hawk is 'really' a handsaw—bah. Humbug. Any creation . . . with any vitality to it, can 'really' be a dozen mutually exclusive things at once."[4] British author and theologian C.S. Lewis makes a similar argument in his review of J.R.R. Tolkien's *Fellowship of the Ring*. Lewis states, "What shows that we are reading myth, not allegory, is that there are no pointers to a specific

. . . application. A myth points, for each reader, to the realm he lives in most. It is a master key: Use it on what door you like."[5] Some critics described Tolkien's work as an allegory about World War II since it was published soon after that harrowing period. Like Lewis, however, John H. Timmerman, author of *Other Worlds: The Fantasy Genre*, argues that, at its core, Tolkien's trilogy is simply a gripping story. Although the narrative can be read as a metaphor for the war that influenced Tolkien's life so profoundly, Timmerman claims that Tolkien would rather us consider that "WWII is a particular manifestation of evil which has occurred in all tribes and tongues and occurs also in fantasy."[6] The story must stand alone, but if peeled back it may reveal a number of deeper levels and meanings.

Of course, the narrative structure of *The Odyssey* is common to more than just fantasy. The idea of heroes overcoming obstacles to arrive at some sort of goal is inherent in nearly all forms of fiction. In fantasy, however, the author is free to abandon many ties to the real world. Monsters or witches can stand in Odysseus's way, or Aladdin, from *The Arabian Nights*, can invoke a magical genie. Such freedom allows fantasy authors to engage their flights of fancy, but it also earmarks their work as fanciful—a tag that would haunt the genre as it progressed into the modern world.

THE ROOTS OF MODERN FANTASY

By the nineteenth century, history had become pigeonholed into three distinct categories: ancient, medieval, and modern. With such a heavy emphasis during this century on realism and science, the medieval period was thought of as the Dark Ages, a backward era with very little intellectual value. Even the ancient civilizations were thought of as superstitious and primitive. Rapid advancements in science, technology, literacy, and even wealth helped fuel the public's thirst for all things rational. It had become unfashionable even to display an interest in the unenlightened times of the past or anything that represented a belief in the fantastic or unexplainable. This trend is clearly represented in the literature of the time. The powerful focus on realism, however, left a gap in the literary market. A few notable authors took advantage of this.

In 1856 William Morris published what is considered by many scholars to be the first true work of modern fantasy.

Writing for a collegiate magazine that he helped to create, Morris published seven pieces of short fantasy. Although these stories are not popularly known today, such as "The Story of the Unknown Church," and "The Hollow Pool," they represent some of the first works to contain the familiar characteristics of modern fantasy. Flying in the face of the current trend toward modernism, these stories placed value on ancient ways of life, the roots of culture, and myth in antiquity. In much of his work, Morris explored England's mythology and retold the stories in modernized tales. Morris went on to publish his first novel in 1886, *A Dream of John Ball*, as well as a number of others, many of which explored utopian fantasy. One of Morris's contemporaries, George MacDonald, was another progenitor of modern fantasy. A theologian, MacDonald penned a book called *Phantastes* in 1858. His subsequent works, along with the works of Morris, were the first attempts at incorporating mythology and a focus on the supernatural into modern fiction writing.

MAGIC

The focus on the supernatural introduced to nineteenth-century readers one of the most ubiquitous elements of fantasy: the invoking of magic. The acceptance of supernatural forces having a direct influence on the day-to-day occurrences of life requires a suspension of disbelief on the part of the reader. Once this surrender occurs, the reader can delve into another level of exploration that pushes the very boundaries of what he or she has come to understand about the way the natural world operates.

Magic is sometimes represented as a natural force, often beyond human control. More often, though, it is presented as a tool to be used by a select group of characters. The tool itself is usually neutral, but the way in which the user wields it is a metaphor for the struggle between good and evil within the characters. The saying "power corrupts" is central to this struggle. What a magus or wizard does with this power, whether he succumbs to his greed and desires or uses it for a nobler purpose, is often at the core of a fantasy story's exploration of morality.

NEW WORLDS

In 1865 a groundbreaking work of surreal fantasy entered the world. Lewis Carroll's *Alice's Adventures in Wonderland* expanded the world of fiction enormously. This story and its companion, *Through the Looking Glass*, exemplified creativity through the convention of free association and made fashionable the contemporary notion of doing "three impossible things before breakfast." It also represented an early exploration of another of the most defining traits of modern fantasy: the exploration of a world that is distinct from the world of the reader. In *Alice's Adventures in Wonderland*, for example, this world exists hidden within the confines of a small grove of "Earthly" woods, but in other fantasy, the "Wonderland" may exist in the same place as the known world but in a different time, or it may simply be a whole new world with absolutely no connection to that of the reader.

Carroll's work was an example of a no-boundaries stampede into the concept of other worlds. Though there is far more meaning to the details of the plot than one might initially think, most of it is not readily apparent to readers. For example, after drinking a potion to make her smaller, and then a cake to make her bigger, Alice becomes frustrated that she cannot find a similar morsel to bring her back to her original size. Eventually she begins fanning herself with the rabbit's discarded fan, and this action makes her begin to rapidly shrink back down. Seemingly, there is no logic to this chain of events. In most works of fantasy, however, there exist obvious rules and order to the other worlds. Good fantasy often hinges on the author's ability to create not only a fresh and different world but also a plausible one. Readers have to be able to grasp the rationale of the other world in order for them to understand the actions of the characters. Discovering the logic of this fictional world is a part of the journey for the reader and, in many cases, the story's protagonist as well.

The attraction of traveling to another world, or even acknowledging its existence, is often described as "escapism." Escapism is the ability to leave the trials and tribulations of the known world behind by entering into a story so fanciful that it has no bearing whatsoever on the events of one's own life or existence. Upon closer examination, however, fantasy literature has no more an element of escapism than any other work of fiction. In fact, good fantasy literature is often based around notions of exploring social, political, personal, and even spiritual issues. Exploring this new world allows readers to reformulate their opinion on any number of things. Rather than escaping, the journey through this other world is often a vehicle for the exploration of questions that have a direct bearing on the real world.

APPROVED FOR ALL AGES

Originally intended as a children's book, *Alice's Adventures in Wonderland*'s depth and intricacies could only truly be appreciated by adults. This was the beginning of a common thread in fantasy: stories that have a dual audience, children and adults. Other so-called children's books of powerful depth, containing rich magic and creativity and tempered by commentary on social, political, and philosophical issues, were being published at the same time. Hans Christian Andersen was publishing fairy tales so rich and multilayered that they seemed to be born out of ancient myth rather than Denmark in the 1800s. His stories, such as "The Little Mermaid" and "The Snow Queen," were engaging tales that also provided commentary on topics such as class struggle, vanity, and love. Along with works such as Italian author Carlo Collodi's *Pinocchio*, a market for adult fantasy was beginning to develop. Not only were the stories gripping enough to excite the adults who read them to their children, but the children of that generation—who were weaned on these stories of the magical and fantastic—grew into adults who craved the same rich imaginative depth in the literature they read. Some critics see the link between children's literature and adult fantasy as one of the firm underpinnings of the modern fantasy genre.

THE COMMON HERO

Whether addressing adults or children, fantasy literature typically has the habit of drawing its reader completely into the story. The stories are often driven by characters who are accessible to the readers. Typically, protagonists are people who start their journeys with significant handicaps. They may be lost and alone, they may be made of wood instead of flesh, or they may simply be ordinary mortals in a playing field of magi and monsters. With the odds stacked against them, they reflect the common, everyday person who struggles through the trials of life. And because of this affinity between the character and the average reader, the reader is not asked to observe a story happening to some mythic superman, so much as to step inside and experience the journey of a character who seems more familiar. L. Frank Baum's *The Wonderful Wizard of Oz*, for example, was based on a simple farm girl from Kansas who embodied traits and a frame of reference that readers could easily relate to as she traveled through the foreign land of good witches and bad witches.

This same concept has remained an integral part of fantasy literature all the way up to the present day. In tales such as David Edding's *The Belgariad*, the naive Garion goes through a process of learning and growth, which transforms him from a common, everyday character into a hero. Garion starts out as a simple farm boy, living a sheltered life with his aunt. As the story unfolds, he is swept away into the intrigues of the world at large, learns to control the elemental forces that drive the world, meets warriors, engages in epic battles, and finally confronts a god in an effort to save the future of his world. Readers are carried along on this journey and are forced to recognize the hero that lays dormant inside them.

GOOD VS. EVIL

As the heroes of fantasy stories travel on their way, they are often confronted with issues and characters that force them to assess the basics of their own views on morality. Many scholars of the genre have noted that a conflict usually exists between the forces representing dark and light, or good and evil. This battle is one that has been waged in real life as well as fiction for as long as humankind has struggled with the notion of morality. What constitutes good and what constitutes evil is a truly subjective judgment. What makes fantasy an effective tool for the exploration of this concept is the fact that the story takes place in completely unfamiliar territory.

In 1950 C.S. Lewis published one of the most enduring and often-read entries in the world of fantasy. *The Lion, the Witch, and the Wardrobe*, the first book in his famous *Chronicles of Narnia* series, represents a very clear picture of this battle. A sharp line is drawn in the sand between the forces of good and the undeniable forces of evil. A theologian, Lewis's books are often ripe with parallels to modern Christianity. For example, Aslan the lion, through his sacrifice and subsequent resurrection, is clearly designed to represent a Christ figure. Other authors may be less blatant, preferring—as in other types of fiction—to more subtly examine the boundaries of the human propensity to wander between the poles of good and evil.

By creating new worlds and weaving a brand new canvas on which to paint the battle between these forces, fantasy authors free the reader of preconceptions and prejudices. Long-standing biases may fall away, and new perspective can be achieved, helping the reader to judge moral standards in a new and objective way. This freedom to think and grow outside of "normalcy," especially when exploring issues as complex as morality, is one of the primary attractions of fantasy literature.

A MEANINGFUL JOURNEY

One of the final fantasy elements is the presence of a quest. From ancient Greek mythology to Tolkien, this basic concept has been at the core of fantasy. Many different types of fiction center around an adventure, but this is not entirely the same thing as a quest. According to Timmerman, an adventure does not necessarily have a specific goal while a quest always does. An adventure can be initiated for any reason, but a quest is usually a spiritual or meaningful undertaking. The quest hero is often appointed or ordained by a higher power. Lastly, an adventure can be whimsical in nature. Although quests may have whimsical elements to them, they are essentially serious endeavors, full of life-threatening challenges around every turn. This formula applies just as well to quaint and classic fantasies, such as Collodi's *Pinocchio,* as it does to modern and graphic ones such as Terry Brooks's *The Sword of Shannara.*

Typically, the quest begins because there is a threat to the status quo. A powerful force is coming to subjugate the local people or even the world, for example. In many cases, the people affected by this are not even aware that it is looming over their heads. An agent of some higher power, or one gifted with a deeper understanding of the natural order of things, must inform the protagonists of the state of affairs and send them on their way. In Robert Jordan's *The Eye of the World* (Book One in his Wheel of Time series), Moiraine, a member of the mysterious female society known as Aes Sedai, arrives in a small rural village to whisk away three young men who may hold the key to the salvation or destruction of their world. Again, this quest is one that typically spans not only geographical terrain but also spiritual terrain. The heroes must explore and discover uncharted regions of their own existence in order to find the strength, wisdom, and constitution to complete their quest. Literary critic Northrop Frye feels that this element of fantasy is one of the central themes of all literature. He states that "all literary genres are derived from the quest myth."[7] Indeed, the concept of the fantastic in literature has been around for quite some time.

WORTHY OR WORTHLESS?

Since J.R.R. Tolkien's *Lord of the Rings* blew the doors of the fantasy market wide open back in the late 1950s and 1960s, the genre has seen a nonstop increase in commercial success. As children were exposed to the surrealism of Tolkien's Middle Earth, their creativity was ignited. Forums for the creation and discussion of fantasy were created in schools and college campuses all over the country. As these "children" came of age, their works carved out a niche in the literary market. Authors such as Ursula K. Le Guin and Terry Brooks borrowed elements of Middle Earth to breathe life into entirely new worlds of their own creation. Other worlds, less tied to Middle Earth, were created as well, such as Piers Anthony's magical land of Xanth—which helped demonstrate that fantasy could mean big dollars for the publishing industry. Today, as entire window displays are dedicated to authors such as J.K. Rowling and Robert Jordan, some critics question the value of such literature. Although many see it as a valuable category of fiction, worthy of the popular acclaim it has received, others see it as simple, mindless fluff. Some detractors have even gone as far as condemning the genre as harmful to the healthy development of young minds.

The harm, some psychologists feel, comes from allowing young people to retreat from the real issues of their world. The escapism offered by works of fantasy is typically seen as a pleasant diversion, but a few psychologists have argued that some people can get lost in these other worlds, choosing to shut off the outside world in favor of these flights of fancy. Although this belief may not be held by a large number of critics and psychologists, it is a concern to some. This concern has existed for some time. As far back as 1888 Ralph Waldo Emerson wrote on the subject of fantasy, saying, "Men live in their fancy like drunkards whose hands are too soft and tremulous for successful labor."[8]

Well-known fantasy author Ursula K. Le Guin agrees that fantasy can have a significant effect on the reader, though she leaves it open to interpret whether that effect is positive or negative. She says, "A fantasy is a journey. It is a journey into the subconscious mind, just as psychoanalysis is. Like psychoanalysis, it can be dangerous; *and it will change you.*"[9]

Proponents of the genre argue that not only isn't fantasy literature dangerous, but it is essential to the stimulation of a person's imagination and creativity. Children often learn the roots of how to think "outside the box" by being exposed to literature that has no boundaries. It is the nurturing of this creative spirit that has led to most of the scientific, medical, and even social advancements of modern society. In all of its many guises—fairy tales, mythology, folklore, and modern fiction—fantasy literature can have a powerful influence on the way people, young or old, look at the world in which they live. As C.S. Lewis put it, "A fairy tale stirs and troubles the child with a sense of something beyond his or her reach, and rather than dulling or emptying the actual world, gives it a new dimension. . . . He does not despise the real woods because he has read of enchanted woods; the reading makes all woods enchanted."[10]

NOTES

1. Richard Matthews, *Fantasy: The Liberation of Imagination.* New York: Twayne, 1997, p. 2.
2. Susan Lehr, "Fantasy: Inner Journeys for Today's Child," *Publishing Research Quarterly,* Fall 1991, p. 96.
3. Lehr, "Fantasy," p. 97.
4. Ursula K. Le Guin, "Dreams Must Explain Themselves," in *Language of the Night,* ed. Susan Wood. New York: G.P. Putnam's Sons, 1979, p. 53.
5. C.S. Lewis, "The Gods Return to Earth," *Time and Tide,* August 15, 1954, p. 1,082.
6. John H. Timmerman, *Other Worlds: The Fantasy Genre.* Bowling Green, OH: Bowling Green State University Popular Press, 1983, p. 9.
7. Northrop Frye, *Fables of Identity: Studies in Poetic Mythology.* New York: Harbinger Books, 1963, p. 17.
8. Ralph Waldo Emerson, "Experience," in *Essays: Second Series.* Philadelphia: David McKay, 1888, p. 69.
9. Ursula K. Le Guin, "From Elfland to Poughkeepsie," in *Language of the Night,* ed. Susan Wood. New York: G.P. Putnam's Sons, 1979, p. 93.
10. C.S. Lewis, "On Three Ways of Writing for Children," in *Of Other Worlds: Essays and Stories,* ed. Walter Hooper. New York: Harcourt, Brace, and World, 1965, p. 29.

CHAPTER 1

Understanding the Fantasy Genre

Fantasy's Roots: Ballads, Folktales, and Legends

Brian Attebery

Brian Attebery, professor of English and philosophy at Idaho State University and author of *The Fantasy Tradition in American Literature*, is a highly respected scholar in the fantasy field. Here he delves into the history of British and American ballads, tall tales, folk stories, fairy tales and legends to chart their metamorphosis into the fantasy fiction of today.

John Greenleaf Whittier, in the collection of curiosities he called *The Supernaturalism of New England,* recounts the story of a family of Irish immigrants in New Hampshire, proprietors of a disastrously unsuccessful tavern. "The landlord," he says, "was a spiteful little man, whose sour, pinched look was a standing libel upon the state of his larder," and the wife was no better, being a scold, a slattern, and a tippler. Nevertheless, their trade suddenly took a turn for the better when a company of Irish fairies took up residence and began holding conversation in the parlor. British fairies, as a rule, abhor both sloppiness and ungenerous dealings, but these may have been lured by voices from home. At any rate, the inn prospered under their influence until the novelty wore off and the crowds once more deserted. Says Whittier: "Had the place been traversed by a ghost, or disturbed by a witch, they could have acquiesced in it very quietly, but this outlandish belief in fairies was altogether an overtask for Yankee credulity.". . . The fairies, "unable to breathe in an atmosphere of doubt and suspicion," . . . promptly departed for greener shores. Whittier himself stands firmly on the side of the unbelieving Yankees, suggesting that the whole incident was an ingenious fraud.

Excerpted from *The Fantasy Tradition in American Literature: From Irving to Le Guin,* by Brian Attebery. Copyright © 1980 by Brian Attebery. Reprinted by permission of Indiana University Press.

Fraud or not, this anecdote suggests a great deal about the nature of Anglo-American folklore. A general trend, since the landing of the Puritans, has been a paring away of the supernatural in those folk genres most amenable to its presence: ballads, tales, and legends. A writer who wishes to produce something both American and fantastic, and who would root his creation, as did the British fantasists, in his native lore, must move against the current, restoring what has been lost over the years or finding eddies of tradition that have resisted the general erosion of the marvelous. . . .

The heyday of British ballad collection was represented in such anthologies as Thomas Percy's *Reliques of Ancient English Poetry* (1765) and Sir Walter Scott's *Minstrelsy of the Scottish Border* (1802–03), both important sources for the scholarly compilation done by Francis James Child (1882–98). A significant number of so-called Child ballads from these and other sources, and some of the most memorable, are built around supernatural episodes and characters, and the treatment given to the uncanny elements is as sober and concrete as that of serious fantasy. M.J.C. Hodgart describes the universe of the ballads as "peopled with animals and birds that speak, with fairies and with ghosts who return from the grave. There is no clear line of demarcation between such creatures and ordinary mortals. The supernatural is treated in a matter-of-fact and unsensational way, and to the ballad singer there seems to be no question of a suspension of disbelief. Fairies, for example, are not the minute creatures of modern whimsy, but are like human beings in size and in some of their ways of life." So important to balladry were the elves and fairies that one of Scott's informants, Margaret Laidlaw, considered them the ballad muses and feared that Scott's writing her songs down would offend them.

Of the English fantasists, Tolkien seems to have been most influenced by traditional ballads. His essay "On Fairy-Stories" makes use of a quotation from one of the most haunting fairy ballads, that of Thomas the Rhymer or "True Thomas.". . . The passage which Tolkien cites to illustrate his conception of the enchanted world of Faerie is the Queen of Elfland's description of the three great roads to Heaven, Hell, and Fairyland. The first is the "path of Righteousness," narrow, thorny, and little used. The second is the "path of Wickedness," broad and lily strewn. The third is neither good nor wicked, merely Other:

And see ye not yon bonny road
  That winds about yon fernie brae?
That is the road to fair Elfland,
  Where thou and I this night maun gae.

Much of the beauty and peril of Tolkien's world is comparable to that of the ballads, and indeed *The Lord of the Rings*
is filled with the ballads of elves and men. The pivotal incident in *The Hobbit,* in which Bilbo Baggins trades riddles
with Gollum at peril of his life, is closely akin to the traditional ballads known as "Riddles Wisely Expounded" and
"The Fause Knight upon the Road,". . . both of which, in their
early forms, tell of mortals saved from death or damnation
by outwitting riddling fiends. The last answer in the former
ballad not only solves the riddle but unmasks the ques-
tioner: "As sune as she the fiend did name, / He flew awa in
a blazing flame."

There are in the ballads a great number of other supernatural motifs available to the writer of fantasy, already presented with the necessary vividness and solidity. Lowry
Charles Wimberly devoted an entire volume to classifying the
supernatural lore of the English and Scottish ballads. He
found treatments of such promising themes as transmigration
of souls, revenants from the grave, otherworld journeys, enchanted forests and caves, fairies, shapeshifters, witches,
spells and enchantments of all varieties, and even a paganized
heaven and hell. Not even a work of the scope of *The Lord of
the Rings* could possibly exhaust the available material. . . .

The interests of the American ballad composer are not
like those of the fantasist but those of the local color writer,
Bret Harte or Mary Hallock Foote, seeking to invest obscure
corners of the nation with "human interest," or the naturalistic documenter, Jack London or Frank Norris, telling with
glum satisfaction of the hardships of some outdoor way of
life. Many American ballads have a strongly journalistic
quality; they subjugate the use of suspense and verbal
artistry to the building up of supportive detail. The folk in
this country seem comparable to the upwardly mobile peas-
ants in Linda Dégh's Hungarian villages: they no longer
wish to hear imaginative impossibilities but prefer something like, and probably based on, a newspaper account.
They do not want to be "fooled" into empathizing with a fiction, still less an outright fantasy.

A partial exception to the general run of American ballads

is the bold, comical, and most definitely fictional account of "Tying a Knot in the Devil's Tail." This is a sort of occupational ballad run wild, in which the skills of two cowhands give them power over the devil himself. The devil in the ballad is spiteful but impotent, rather like the unfortunate devil who steals "The Farmer's Curst Wife" in the Child ballad of that name. In this case the supernatural is treated as a joke. There is no question of belief, of "paying something extra," in E.M. Forster's terms; rather the effect is to forestall any subsequent efforts to create a serious story around the devil or any other traditional non-human being. Humor acts to defuse the sense of wonder that marks fantasy. If there is to be humor in a work of fantasy, it must be kept separate from the component of the marvelous, as Tolkien isolates the often bumptious hobbits from the stern and magical elves. Mixing simple cowboys and fallen angels, without any mediating characters or principles, can only produce the ludicrous incongruity effectively exploited by this ballad.

"Tying a Knot in the Devil's Tail" has more in common with the tall tale, which is a particular form of the folktale, than with other ballads. Tales, like ballads, thrive best in regions of little literacy, where they need not compete with the written word. In this country, the tale and the ballad are found most commonly in the Southern mountains, from Virginia to Missouri, where isolation and poverty have allowed an oral culture to continue relatively undisturbed. Folksong as a popular mode of entertainment, however, was not seriously challenged by mass communication until the development of electronic recording and broadcasting, whereas folk literature found itself in direct competition with popular journals and newspapers early in the nineteenth century. The long narrative forms like the fairy tale, requiring a skilled narrator and a willing audience, tended to be replaced in our oral tradition by shorter, simpler forms like the tall tale or the joke, and jokes themselves became briefer and more dependent on the punch line and the quick laugh.

In most places where long folktales are still told, wonder tales or *Märchen* form an important part of the repertoire. England is not noted for its *Märchen* as are the Celtic, Scandinavian, and Central European countries, but fine versions of such tales as "Beauty and the Beast," "Cinderella," and "The Juniper Tree" have been collected there. The *Type and Motif Index of the Folktales of England and North America* lists greater numbers of *Märchen* types here than in the parent country, but its compiler, Ernest W. Baughman, suggests that the American variants reflect an earlier stage in English tradition. American storytellers, more isolated than their English cousins, preserve more of the old tales, just as they preserve older songs or forms of speech. As with ballads, though, the stories have undergone Americanization.

Settings in the American folktales are adapted to the frontier scene; they are full of forested hills and cleared fields. As Richard Chase has pointed out, even the kings and giants who carry over from Europe live in log houses and spend their time breaking "newground." The hero of one cycle of stories, Jack, is less a fairy tale hero than a classic American trickster, adaptable and unscrupulous, a local boy who gets by on his wits without supernatural aid. Some of the Jack tales veer from *Märchen* to tall tale, as when Jack goes hunting and takes a full bag with a single bullet. . . .

Most susceptible to the process of rationalization are the nonhuman figures of the European *Märchen*. A few witches survive, and some scaled-down giants, but the evil magician tends to blur into the comic devil we have already met in ballads, and the only dragon evident is altered almost beyond recognition into the "Old Fire Dragoman," a pipe-smoking old man with an ogreish temperament. . . .

A typical treatment is the variant of "The Three Wishes" collected in Arkansas by Vance Randolph. In it the three wishes are given to a foolish old couple and promptly wasted, as in European versions, but the emphasis in the story is shifted from the magical possibilities to pragmatic considerations. The ham produced by the first unintentional wish is not wasted but carefully wished back on the plate. Whereas the magic in the European tale serves to illustrate a fine array of ironies involving greed, this American retelling blurs the message by informing us that hocus-pocus, and not the basic motivation, was at fault:

> So pretty soon the old man went down to the road, and there was a letter in the box. It was from their married daughter, and she had sent them some money. She says there is plenty more where that came from, as her man has got a good job now. So it looks like everything turned out all right after all, even if the old folks did make a mess of them three wishes. . . .

Stories which are given credence by tellers and hearers are known to folklorists as legends. Actually, a legend may often be told by a skeptic, but always with an awareness that someone somewhere—old-timer, child, churchgoer, or "gentile"—maintains its truth. As I mentioned before, a primary source for English fantasy is the vast and colorful body of fairy legend. Katharine Briggs has cataloged the major tribes of fairy folk in British belief, from the piksies of Cornwall to the *siths* of the Highlands. Among them a fantasist can find supernatural beings great or small, beautiful or grotesque, benevolent or threatening, to weave into his story. The fairy tradition also holds that uncounted mortals have slipped from our world to Elfland, and the lucky ones back again: the path from England to the Other World is a well-worn one. But American storytellers have dropped the fairies from their repertoires, with the result that fairyland—that is, the entire realm of Faërie or enchantment—has become distant and abstract, no longer the glittering hall under the next mountain. The disappearance of supernatural beings is characteristic not only of Anglo-American culture, but of all European immigrant groups: "Irish-Americans remember the fairies. Norwegian-Americans the *nisser,* Greek-Americans the *vrykólakas,* but only in relation to events remembered in the Old Country. . . . Apparently the ethnic supernatural figures are too closely associated with the culture and geography of the Old Country to migrate."

Some of the fairy folk set out to emigrate to this country. Katharine Briggs recounts the story of a family, plagued by a household goblin, who decided to escape to America. As they start to leave, they inform a neighbor of their plans, and a voice from the churn pipes in, "Aye George, we're flitting." But neither that cheerfully malevolent sprite nor any of his kind, save perhaps Whittier's woeful Irish fairies, ever showed up in our tradition. Their lack leaves our rivers and hills curiously empty: we may explore or exploit them but never meet their spirits face to face.

America is not without legends, however. Richard Dorson classifies American legend into four phases: the colonial period, dominated by religious beliefs; the early national period, when regional heroes represented a new democratic faith; the later national period, a time of economic and occupational lore; and the contemporary period, marked by druglore and counter-culture protest. . . .

Sentimental fairy verse appeared in many of the popular literary periodicals of the early nineteenth century, often under pseudonyms, as if the authors felt they were conde-scending. John Milton Harney (calling himself merely "An American") published his *Crystalina: A Fairy Tale* as early as 1816. William Gibson's *A Vision of Faery Land* did not appear until 1853. Throughout this period, and even later, there appears the same overly precious treatment of the subject. In some poems, the fairies become mere decoration; in others, a clever conceit. S.G. Goodrich, for example, uses certain connotations of the word *fairy*—tininess, bright colors, speed—to create a mock parable of the "Birthnight of the Humming Birds," in which a tribe of Irish fairies come to America to hunt jewels, get caught by the sunrise, and are permanently transformed. This is neither legend nor fantasy, but rather an extended form of the same kind of whimsy that makes Emily Dickinson describe the hummingbird's wings as a "fairy gig," a whimsy that she abandons in her later and stronger poem on the same subject.

These mannered fairy poems represent an attempt to fill a gap in American tradition, a gap first felt, seemingly, not by the folk but by professional writers. Drake and the rest tried, by means of a set of borrowed poetic devices two steps removed from living folk tradition, to interpret the American landscape, which seemed to them, in contrast with Europe, empty and spiritless. They created neither a lasting art nor a viable legendry. A writer with more skill, more awareness of real traditional materials, and a little luck could, however, transfer European motifs to an American setting and produce something quite as memorable as legend. William Austin's "Peter Rugg, the Missing Man," for example, is a Massachusetts Flying Dutchman, a man condemned by an ill-advised oath to race around New England in the teeth of a great storm in a vain attempt to get to Boston by nightfall. The hard-edged realism of the story, as opposed to the moonlit fuzziness of the fairy poems, renders it eerily effective: the supernatural is all the more powerful for being played against a backdrop of solid New England practicality.

Another American character who becomes unstuck in time (is that a particular national fear?) is at the center of our best-known literary legend, "Rip Van Winkle." Washington Irving's story has been retold, versified, dramatized, and painted enough times to suggest that Rip has fixed himself securely in the American consciousness, even though Irving took his theme, not from American, but from German traditional sources. Irving himself comments on the similarity of Van Winkle's adventures to stories attached to Frederick Barbarossa, one of many sleeping heroes scattered around Europe. Once again scenery and characterization work to naturalize the import. And Irving's sharp eye and deftness of style allow him to orchestrate a legend of much greater complexity than "Peter Rugg." Indeed, Irving brought the fairies to America, in the guise of Hendrick Hudson and the crew of the Half-moon. Hudson, with his confused nationality and his mysterious disappearance, carries just the right air of antiquity and strangeness to act the role of demigod in that part of the world he claimed for the Dutch. By selecting the old explorer, rather than some conventional, diminutive fairy king, Irving recaptures the danger and grotesquery of the best European narratives. We are never sure whether the silent carousers are ghosts or nature spirits bowling thunder in the mountains. They might be good or evil or mockingly indifferent. Whatever the case, they are formidable and alien, and Rip is lucky to have escaped at the loss of only twenty years of his life—especially after violating the traditional tabu against eating and drinking in the Other World.

The mountain hollow where Rip's adventure takes place is indeed a fairyland in miniature, and "Rip Van Winkle" is as much fantasy as literary legend. Its plot line is easily translated into the terms of Propp's morphology: interdiction (Dame Van Winkle orders Rip out of Nicholas Vedder's tavern), lack (Rip's lack of a happy home), departure (the hunting trip), acquisition of a magical agent (appearance of Hudson and his men), transference to a designated place (entry into the amphitheater), contest (the drinking bout), branding or marking the hero (Rip's sudden aging), liquidation of misfortune or lack (Dame Van Winkle's death), return of the hero, unrecognized arrival, and, finally, recognition of the hero. There is no final wedding and accession to the throne, because Rip's tale is one of abdication rather than assumption of responsibility. . . .

Irving demonstrates that the writer can transcend his store of traditional materials. If he is sensitive to the dynamics of his native lore, he can revise it, rearrange it, and insert motifs from other cultures, where they will not strain the basic fabric. But it is not an easy operation: Irving himself managed it with such success only once, and "Rip Van Winkle" is only a sketch. It takes place in a tiny corner of the country, among a people not yet assimilated to American life; yet even among those isolated Dutchmen there is skepticism toward Rip's story, especially among the younger and more prosperous members of the community. Were the tale to trespass beyond its geographical and temporal limits, entering into modern mercantile America, the delicate blend of magic and humor would be undone. What passes in the haunted Catskills would never survive New York City. Irving shows how American fantasy can be created, but not how it can be made full scale, nor how the sense of wonder may spread to the broader American scene.

Our folk songs, stories, and beliefs, especially our beliefs, portray a population increasingly pragmatic and impatient, interested mostly in the here and now, susceptible to sentimentality, but only if convinced that its tears are being jerked by real events. If the dark vision of the Puritans still haunts us in our midnight dreams, that is all the more reason for scoffing in the daylight. Most of our popular literature falls into the same pattern: indeed, the line is thin between the broadside ballad and the newspaper eulogy, or the oral and written tall tale. Both kinds of narrative, folk and popular, have shaped American habits of expectation and belief and have created a serious problem for the artist, Irving or even Drake, who wishes to reach beyond practical concerns and the limits of daily existence.

Fantasy Literature Both Reflects and Denies Reality

Jules Zanger

Jules Zanger is a professor of English at Southern
Illinois University at Edwardsville and author of
many articles on literary criticism. In this piece, he
contends that fantasy is a unique genre in that it
must reflect and deny reality at the same time. He
uses the category of heroic fantasy (later known as
high fantasy) to demonstrate how fantasy writers use
the elements of the genre to achieve a wondrous alternate world that feels as authentic as the real one.

Each kind of literature retains for its own purposes certain
aspects of reality and denies certain others. Realism and naturalism, for example, are defined by those elements of the
real world they retain; fantasy, on the other hand, is defined
by those aspects of reality it denies, by representations that
are not merely improbable or untrue, as are common to all
fictions, but patently false.

That reality, both the physical reality of experience and
the conventionalized reality of literature, provides the foil
against which fantasy defines itself. Unlike other literary
modes which, to be effective, traditionally require the "suspension of disbelief," fantasy requires the reader's disbelief,
his recognition that the fiction is not real, to achieve its nature as fantasy.

The base line of reality, therefore, is always implicit in
even the most errant fantasy, and in the tension between
those solid, familiar, unalterable givens of experience and
the particular denials of them that constitute the fiction is
generated the special delight that fantasy affords us.

Reprinted by permission of the publisher from "Heroic Fantasy and Social Reality: *Ex
nihilo nihil fit*," by Jules Zanger, in *The Aesthetics of Fantasy Literature and Art*, edited
by Roger C. Schlobin. Copyright © 1982 by University of Notre Dame Press.

CREATING OTHER WORLDS

The airiest of fantasies created by the writer's imagination is always firmly staked to the bedrock provided by the reader's knowledge and experience of reality. Each fantasy takes its distinctive shape from those aspects of the real world it most strongly rejects. The roots of fantasy are to be found, then, not mainly in myth nor in the collective unconscious nor the spillage of a frustrated psyche, but in the denial of real human experience taking place in real historical time.

Fantasy offers an alternative vision, a critique, and the basis of opposition to that real world. The author's private vision, when written, becomes public and socialized, contrived to embody and reinforce the private fantasies of its readers. To the extent that those private fantasies are conformable into the literary fantasy—and that the literary fantasy succeeds in crystallizing and giving hard artifactual shape to the daydreams and undisciplined imaginings of the public—that fantasy is rooted in the social experience of the real world. Fantasy, consequently, always exists in a symbiotic relationship with reality and its conventionalized representation, depending on it for its existence and at the same time commenting upon it, criticizing it, and illuminating it.

Since fantasy springs (but not very far) from the denial of aspects of the real world, the distance between that real world and the world created by the fantasist reveals those stress points at which the real world chafes the writer and reader, and chafing, generates the imaginative alternative, as the grain of sand generates the baroque pearl.

[Writer] Loren Eiseley suggests in his essay, "The Lethal Factor," that this ability to create the imaginative alternative is one of the quantum steps that distinguishes human beings from beasts: "The *mundus alter*—this other intangible, faery world of dreams, fantasies, inventions—has been flowing through the heads of men since the first ape-man succeeded in cutting out a portion of his environment and delineating it in a transmissible word." The human mind, that is, in its ability to imagine an existence other than the one which it experiences, is permitted to perceive, as if from the outside, the existence in which it actually is immersed. The ability to create fantasy permits us to create history. But fantasy is not merely the creation of a *"mundus alter,"* an alternative to the real world; any reality can have an almost infinite number of alternatives. Fantasy is a response to a particular combination of historical conditions. When, however, we have a significant number of literary works that share as their primary characteristic similar violations of the limits of possible experience, we have a literary convention, a genre of fantasy which itself shapes subsequent fantasies. The particular fantasy, then, at one time violates the known and shared parameters of reality, and observes and reinforces the expectations established by the genre.

To suggest, as does [fantasy scholar] W.R. Irwin, that fantasies violate norms is only half the story; fantasies also perpetuate norms. [Fellow scholar] Eric Rabkin suggests that fantasies involve the reversals of expectation, but that reversal in fantasy is precisely what is the expected. The magical apparition that turns out to have been produced by real trapdoors and mirrors is as inappropriate a reversal in a fantasy as a solution to a locked door mystery of John Dickson Carr's that depends on the villain passing through the keyhole in a puff of smoke.

Fantasy's denials, violations, or reversals all occur within the circumscribed limits of the genre; they must be considered not only in terms of what reality leads us to expect, but, more significantly, in terms of what the genre leads us to expect. To treat each fantasy as if it were the first of its kind is to ignore the highly conventionalized nature of its form and content. The one expectation that cannot be negated is that some expectation will be negated. If this expectation is denied, we have realism, not fantasy.

Though these denials of reality define the fiction as fantasy, they normally constitute only a small portion of the total fiction, embedded in it like plums in the pudding of the familiar. Once we accept the denial of the real world implicit in magic that works, or the existence of elves, or the possibility of talking flowers, we find ourselves on otherwise familiar turf: conflict and resolution, psychological characterization, and motivation all seem relatively undistinguishable from that found in the historical romance. Good and evil remain definable and familiar. George MacDonald, writing of this retained ground base of fantasy, was essentially correct when he observed, "In physical things a man may invent; in moral things he must obey—and take their laws with him into his invented world as well."

BUILDING ON FAMILIAR EXPERIENCES

Fantasies consist, then, of retentions as well as denials, taken from the context of familiar experience and from a literary convention which is part of that familiar experience.

A number of important forms of fantasy emerge from this experience. One is that kind in which the reader is intended to read the fiction as a more or less thinly disguised commentary on the social situation in which he lives. We immediately think of that whole class of utopian or satiric fantasy—from Aristophanes' *The Birds,* to Swift's *Gulliver's Travels,* to Orwell's *Animal Farm*—that invites the reader to read with a kind of double vision, recording the details of the fantasy world and decoding them into their recognizable real world equivalents. Other forms of fantasy have no such programmatic, conscious, organizing principle. Instead, they rely more heavily on literary models, or variations, which appear to have little systematic relationship to reality. Nevertheless, even in those fantasies least clearly linked to the familiar world of experience or to existing models, the careful reader can discover in the value structure, in the characterizations, even in the imagery and metaphor, evidence of the social situation that the fantasy retains and transforms. The different values placed on chastity—for example, in Spenser's *Faerie Queene* where it is the *sine qua non* of femininity and in Michael Moorcock's *Gloriana* where the same chaste queen that Spenser celebrated couples frequently, casually, and innocently with men, women, and beasts—tell us a great deal about the respective societies that generated them. Fantasy's roots in social reality are to be discovered, then, in both its denials and its retentions.

The possible variations of fantasy in terms of denials and retentions are immense. Unlike lyric poetry or tragedy or the detective story, fantasy is not a self-contained literary type. Because it skirts between high art and pulp fiction, because it emerged and flourishes without the significant benefits of academic commentary, and because its efflorescence has been so wild and gorgeous, it invites and resists the most painstaking classifications.

HEROIC FANTASY CREATES ITS OWN REALITY

The relationships of fantasy to social reality are best illustrated in that body of writing popularly called fantasy that emerged in the latter part of the nineteenth century, experienced an astonishing rebirth in the 1950s with the appearance of the Tolkien trilogy, and proliferated into the present. This continuing literary type, though it by no means employs all the possibilities of fantastic writing, represents perhaps the greatest number of the fantasies that have been written and read, and the greatest part of those works customarily identified as fantasies in the checklists and bibliographies of the genre. I am referring, of course, to that type of writing normally designated "heroic fantasy" or "high fantasy," which contains not only the pulp extravaganzas of the "sword-and-sorcery" school but also most of the great familiar classics of fantasy writing from George MacDonald, William Morris, and Lord Dunsany to such contemporary masters as J.R.R. Tolkien and Michael Moorcock. Despite the variety of differences we can find even within this limited type, the great body of heroic fantasy reveals a shared set of romantic characteristics that suggest the highly conventional nature of this form.

Primary among these is the locating of the narrative in a setting that is vaguely medieval, combining the matter of chivalry and of the fairy tale to produce the representative temporal and geographical locus of heroic fantasy. Drawing on the romantic impulses that so infused the work of Sir Walter Scott and John Keats and the contemporary Pre-Raphaelite Brotherhood and on the remarkably pervasive Fairy Books of Andrew Lang, heroic fantasy emerged in the writing of William Morris and George MacDonald, combining romantic adventure, innocent eroticism, and a sense of wonder. Its world was pre-industrial, pre-national, and pre-technological, fixed roughly by its swords and castle keeps and costumes in the Middle Ages. This model of fantasy offered a society of aristocratic, hierarchical order, but it is such an order at a time of emergence or close to breakdown. It resembles the American frontier world in that at very short distances from its civil centers, chaos and wonder and danger await or intrude. Threatened as it is by forces of evil, it is frequently also only a short temporal distance from chaos and old night. It is neither a peaceful nor a secure world, and the representative fantasy customarily involves the overcoming of the threat of evil and the establishment of order through acts of individual confrontation and personal courage.

One significant characteristic that distinguishes the world of heroic fantasy from that of the historic Middle Ages is the absence of the Church as an institution of power and significance. When C.S. Lewis, in *The Chronicles of Narnia,* chose to write Christian allegory in the mode of heroic fantasy, he was constrained to substitute pagan elements for those Christian elements that would have been inappropriate to the mode. Heroic fantasy exists in an essentially pagan world within which only minor and local rulers and deities preside, a state strikingly illustrated by Fritz Leiber's highly popular Fafhrd and the Gray Mouser series.

It is a fragmented world of many boundaries and frontiers, the crossing of which seems to be as inevitable for its protagonists as it is dangerous. For this reason, maps have become standard accompaniments to heroic fantasies, not because they impart any verisimilitude, since that is never the intention of fantasy, but rather because they illustrate graphically the fragmentation of the fantastic world, and the binding, base-touching aspect of the quest the protagonists customarily pursue. Each frontier offers a new landscape, a new folk, a new testing, or a new alliance. Heroic fantasies demand borders and frontiers because the heroic action customarily begins with the crossing of borders, the violation of the limits of the familiar to enter that *mundus alter* that is just over the mountain or across the running brook. For example, the world-wide meanderings of Robert E. Howard's barbarian Conan through the varied locales of the Hyborian Age are limited only by his vague goal of discovering a fabled golden city.

The most representative denial of the real world that takes place in heroic fantasy is the presence of magic that works, and with such magic, all of its extensions: demons, wizards, elves, goblins, trolls, dragons, and supernatural creatures from traditional folk and fairy tales or transformed versions of them—all of those things, that is, that science and normal experience deny existence to. Without this particular denial, heroic fantasy becomes merely historical romance, a literary type that offers its own particular denials of reality, but never as forthrightly as does fantasy. The presence of magic is most often one of the givens of the fantastic world, so that elves and wizards are as strange as, but no stranger than, Roumanians, for example, or native-born New Yorkers. The protagonists may be astonished at encountering them, but not at their existence. Magic distinguishes heroic fantasy from historical romance, but its function in the fantasy is frequently to be defeated. "Good" magic rarely defeats "bad" magic. Good magicians are frequently—like Gandalf imprisoned in Moria, or Merlin under Nimue's spell, or Schmendrick in Peter Beagle's *The Last Unicorn* (and even, most memorably, the Wizard of Oz)—unavailable, preoccupied, or simply inept. Evil magic is defeated finally by human virtues: courage, skill, innocence, or love.

In fairy tales, magic is part of the natural order. Oberon's realm only incidentally coincides with the world of human affairs and has its own purposes and its own bounds. Magic in heroic fantasy, however, frequently involves a disbalancing of the natural order; the evil magician is employing abilities not properly human in the service of an all-too-human appetite for power, which exercises itself primarily in destroying the human community. In this sense, magic in the heroic fantasy, unlike magic in the folk or fairy tale, which usually involves personal and discrete encounters, has a political and social dimension, concerning itself with kingdoms today and the world tomorrow. It is appropriate, then, that the defeat of evil magic is accomplished by human characters or their representatives in the fantasy. Seen this way, high fantasy dramatizes the successful resistance of heroic individuals to faceless power, the successful resistance of the familiar, personal world to the impersonal forces that would alter or destroy it. In this regard, G.K. Chesterton observed, "Magic was the abuse of preternatural powers by lower agents whose work was preternatural but not supernatural; it was founded on the profound maxim of *diabolus simius Dei;* the Devil is the ape of God. . . . There is in enchantment almost always an idea of captivity. In contrast with this it will be noted that the good miracles, the acts of saints and heroes, are always acts of restoration." This emphasis on restoration or retention of a cherished past is particularly important in heroic fantasy, which always seeks its Golden Age in some earlier time. For this reason, the quest for the True King, the concern for legitimacy, which is nothing more than consonance with the past, emerges as a dominant theme in fantasy. This pattern reveals itself in the confirmatory ceremony of *The Sword in the Stone,* in all the paraphernalia of the past fleshing out the Tolkien trilogy and culminating in *The Return of the King,* and, at its most elaborate, the Ritual of the Investiture of the seventy-seventh Earl of Groan in Mervyn Peake's *Titus Groan.*

NATURALISM, HIGH FANTASY, AND VICTORIAN IDEOLOGY

This pattern of fantasy, though it had earlier analogs, emerges in the last decades of the nineteenth century and is almost exactly contemporaneous with naturalism, which affirmed the inability of men and women to shape their destinies. In a sense, high fantasy can be regarded as the mirror image of naturalism, celebrating the triumph of human imagination over brutalizing fact. Naturalism regarded humanity in the aggregate, as controlled by huge, impersonal forces that finally could not be resisted. High fantasy offered a uniquely personal world in which individuals could triumph over incredible odds, in which the traditional virtues—love, decency, courage, innocence—were somehow adequate to maintain the balance of Victorian values against a rapidly tilting universe. In an industrial, urbanized age in which individuality seemed endangered and human centrality lost in the infinite universe revealed by science, fantasy reduced the world to a conceivable dimension. Fantasy restored the primacy of the romantic imagination, providing a world which, if not man-centered, was at least confrontable.

This traditional world of heroic fantasy, rich in the conventional signs of its kind—castle keeps, desolate wastes, princesses, supernatural evils and, of course, heroes—emerged as a popular English literary mode in the work of George MacDonald and William Morris, both of whom represent Victorian sensibility at its most divided. Each was an intensely public man—Morris an extremely successful manufacturer, craftsman/artist, and energetic advocate of Socialism; and MacDonald a popular novelist and popular lecturer on subjects as diverse as chemistry, English literature, physics, and Christianity. Both turned to fantasy as it offered imaginative alternatives to the utilitarian world of hard fact and to Victorian bourgeois commodity culture. In a society in which rampant economic individualism prevailed, they created a past in which they could discover fragmented worlds achieving community through transcendent rather than material goals, communities linked together by what Thomas Carlyle called "organic filaments." They constructed this world of elements taken from Spenser and Malory, from the Arthurian cycle, from the idealized medievalism of the literary past, precisely as Spenser and Malory had turned to the idealized medievalism of still earlier writers. High fantasy offered a universe of imaginative possibility rather than of limiting fact, of a green and rural England rather than one of festering urban slums, of a hierarchical, ordered society rather than one racked by the profound social disorders created by an industrial revolution for which there existed no precedent. Fantasy permitted the laissez-faire individualism of the period to be retained but transformed it into a heroic idealism. The goal of Disraeli and the "Young England" party to establish a coalition of aristocracy and the lower classes against the middle class bourgeoisie was achieved in heroic fantasy by the simple device of creating a world in which the middle class had never emerged as an important force. A significant exception to this occurs in William Morris's *The Well at the World's End,* where the focus of villainy is precisely the burghers, who are cold, grasping, and "doubled-led." Lionel Trilling, writing of another eminent Victorian, Matthew Arnold, observed that "much of what man does for himself depends upon what society permits him to do." Fantasy envisioned a world in which the individual was permitted to act with a directness and immediacy denied him in the conventional bureaucratic structures of commercial, industrial society. The same impulses that led to the mass adulation of such public personalities as mountain climbers, cricket stars, and explorers brought readers to heroic fantasy, that afforded an imaginative release from the drab world of the Victorians.

In its reifying of a magical world, heroic fantasy moved its readers back to their own childhoods, to nursery stories and fairy tales and the innocent wonder they provided, and to the satisfying vision of innocence they made briefly possible. But on another level, magic in heroic fantasy is presented as power that decrees rather than petitions, that is opaque and incomprehensible, and that is as threatening to traditional values as the technological, industrial, and social changes England was undergoing. The defeat of such magic in heroic fantasy can be understood, then, as the symbolic expression of Victorian ambivalence toward progress and change. The Crystal Palace, raised as it were by magic and filled with the mechanical wonders of the age, was as seductive and alluring as Spenser's Castle Joyeuse, but to the discerning eye, as false and as ultimately evil.

Another indication of this unease in the presence of social change is illustrated vividly in one particular pattern of imagery that emerges repeatedly in heroic fantasy. The forces of evil—from George MacDonald's Goblins in *The Princess and the Goblin* to Alan Garner's bodachs in *The Moon of Gomrath*, from Tolkien's Orcs in the Ring trilogy to such more recent versions as Joy Chant's trolls in *Red Moon and Black Mountain* and Marion Zimmer Bradley's Ironfolk in *The House Between the Worlds*—take the shape of deformed dwellers underground who emerge into the world of sunlight to overthrow established order. In all of these works, the reader's sympathy is won to support an aristocratic, pastoral world whose rulers are benevolent and supernaturally supported over and beyond the forces of dark magic arrayed against them. This pattern of imagery is not confined to heroic fantasy, of course. It is to be found in this period in fantasies as diverse as H.G. Wells's *The Time Machine* and Arthur Machen's "The Novel of the Black Seal" and Kenneth Grahame's *The Wind in the Willows*. These deformed subterranean dwellers may have had their origins in the legends of such aboriginal dwellers in the land as the Daione Sidhe of Ireland or the Tylwyth Teg of Wales, but their contemporary application was made clear and fixed by George MacDonald when he described his Goblins as follows:

> There was a legend current in the country, that at one time they lived above ground, and were very like other people. But for some reason or other, concerning which there were very different legendary theories, the king had laid what they thought too severe taxes upon them, or had required observances of them they didn't like, or had begun to treat them with more severity, in some way or other, and impose stricter laws, and the consequence was that they had all disappeared from the face of the country. According to the legend, however, instead of going to some other country, they had all taken refuge in the subterranean caverns. . . . Those who had caught sight of them said that they had greatly altered in the course of generations: and no wonder, seeing they had lived away from the sun, in wet and dark places. They were now, not ordinarily ugly, but either absolutely hideous, or ludicrously grotesque both in face and form.

H.G. Wells was to describe the origins of his underground dwellers, the Morlocks, less romantically, but in essentially the same terms: "So, in the end, above ground you must have the Haves, pursuing pleasure and comfort and beauty, and below ground the Have-Nots, the Workers getting continually adapted to the conditions of their labour." Emerging as it did following half a century of economic unrest and class violence, heroic fantasy offered the images of evil in shapes that resonated with the nightmares of the middle-class audience for which it was written as well as of its middle-class creators.

When Thomas Carlyle described the Chartist rioters in the Manchester insurrection as "a million-headed hydra" driven by cavalry back "into its subterranean settlements again," he was anticipating the imagery of almost a century of fantasy to follow. The pale and stunted miners and mill operatives were finally suppressed by armed force, but they still rise to haunt the fantasies we read.

The creators of high fantasy offered to their readers a *mundus alter* that resolutely denied the most pressing and problematical aspects of their real world, but never forgot any of them. These denials of reality were rooted in an acute sensitivity to that world's failure to provide beauty, order, and community. This disappointment generated fantasies that at their worst were sentimental escapism combined with a strong absence of any democratic feeling; at their best they offered imaginative alternatives to reality that embody ideal solutions to problems that are otherwise uncontrollable. Their banalities and their excellences are, of course, the products of individual authors who bring to the form their own particular impress, who make it, for worse or better, their own. The matter they work on, however, is the social reality they share with their readers. Lord Dunsany was aware of this, of course, when he wrote the following preface to *The King of Elfland's Daughter:*

> I hope that no suggestion of any strange land that may be conveyed by the title will scare readers away from this book; for, though some chapters do indeed tell of Elfland, in the greater part of them there is no more to be shown than the face of the fields we know, and ordinary English woods and a common village and valley, a good twenty or twenty-five miles from the border of Elfland.

The Building Blocks of Fantasy

Susan Dexter

Susan Dexter, the author of nine fantasy novels, recognizes that certain elements can be found in all fantasy fiction. In order for a book to successfully qualify as a fantasy, an author needs to recognize the "building blocks" that form the backbone of the genre. The writer must study folklore and mythology, and be able to accurately craft a realistic new world, complete with names for the characters and maps of their journeys.

Fantasy is the oldest form of literature—the great umbrella that arches over *all* fiction. Fantasy is also a marketing category, shelved and intermingled with science fiction, wearing scaly dragons on its covers in place of shiny spaceships. Fantasy's themes spring from the collective unconscious. Fantasy is populated by archetypes and demons common to us all. Our dreams and our nightmares. Fairy tales.

It's *hard* to be original in this genre. But limits are illusions. Consider: We have but 26 letters in our alphabet. And they'd best be used in combinations readers will recognize as *words*. Now, *there's* a limit. Music? Even worse, but composers don't seem to mind that there are only so many notes to go around.

"Never been done before" may truly be impossible. But "Never been done like *that* before"? That sounds like a goal to me. *Star Wars* didn't wow the world because it was a *new* idea; it resonates with audiences because it's a very *old* story: a fairy tale, right down to the princess. Retell an old tale—do it in a fresh way, and your readers will gasp in wonder. Do it well, and you'll have editors drooling.

Reprinted from "Tricks of the Wizard's Trade," by Susan Dexter, *The Writer*, November 1997. Reprinted with permission from the author.

RESEARCH FANTASY'S ORIGINS

The first trick in a wizard's bag is this: Look at your sources of inspiration. Be a *reader*, before you begin to write. Read new fantasies. Keep up with the field. Read the classics. Comic books aren't forbidden fruit—just don't make them an exclusive diet. Read fairy tales. Read folklore. Study the magic and mythologies of many cultures. If you feed your subconscious properly, it will supply your storytelling needs.

Go to your public library. Breathe in the fresh air and book dust. Surf the Net later. No need to memorize the Dewey System to graze the shelves productively. The 200's are philosophy and religion—*all* religions. Folklore lives in the 398.2's—right next to the prettified fairy tales "retold for children." You'll find original folk tales that will make your hair stand on end and get your juices flowing. Nancy Arrowsmith's *Field Guide to the Little People* will convince you that elves are neither Disney critters nor the fantasy analogue of Vulcans, but beings far more ancient and interesting. *The Golden Bough,* James George Frazer's study of myth and religion, supplied the magical system my wizard Tristan used in *The Ring of Allaire* and its two sequels. I doubt that a thousand authors mining day and night could exhaust that book's possibilities.

Remember the hero has a *thousand* faces. If you confine your reading to role-playing manuals, the stirring high fantasy you hope to craft will be a pale, weak thing, a fifth-generation videotape. Recycled characters stuck in a plot that's a copy of an imitation of J.R.R. Tolkien won't excite an editor these days. Read to understand what the classic themes are. Tolkien based *The Lord of the Rings* solidly on the northern European mythic tradition. It's not a copy of anything, but we respond to it as something familiar.

THE IMPORTANCE OF ACCURACY

Fantastic elements work only if you make *reality* real. If I carelessly give my horses "paws," will you believe what I tell you about dragons? So think about the nuts and bolts, and don't trust Hollywood to do it for you. Castles—where did people *live* in them? Surely everyone wasn't born a princess. Who grows the food, does the laundry, cleans up after the knights' horses? When you research actual medieval cultures, you'll turn up truths far stranger than anything you could *invent.* Your characters should have real lives, with routines, habits, responsibilities. Most of us have to work for a living, and while being a princess may be a full-time job, being an elf is not. My title character in *The Wind-Witch* stands out from the pack of fantasy heroines: Not only is she *not* a princess, but she has a job—two jobs: She's a farmer and a weaver. Getting her sheep through lambing season matters just as much to Druyan as warding off a barbarian invasion or discovering her magical talents. That makes her *real*, for all that she can literally whistle up a storm. Readers can identify with her.

Magic was the science of its day. Science is of fairly recent origin. Both science and magic seek to explain and control the natural world, usually for a man's benefit. Study belief systems. Decide what suits your story, and stick to that. Don't throw in random demons just because they sound cool. Plan your world, if you want it to work for you.

Maps are more than endpaper decorations, and you should start drawing one before you ever start writing your fantasy. Never mind your quest-bound characters: A map will keep *you*, the author, from getting lost. If the desperate ride from Castle A to Castle B takes three days, then the trip back from B to A can take *longer* once the pressure's off; but if the journey takes *less* time, you have major explaining to do. Maps can spare you such *faux pas*.

Maps can suggest plot solutions. In the real world, things are where they are for good reasons. Castles protect and are not built where there's nothing worth contesting. Towns are tied to trade; they grow where roads cross, beside safe harbors. As I began to write *The Wind-Witch*, I had established in an earlier book that my Esdragon had a cliffy coast and treacherous seas. Now I needed it to suffer an invasion—by sea. Where could the invaders strike? Well, the Eral are after plunder, so they want towns. And Esdragon's towns—as in the real-world town of Cornwall, on which I based my fictional duchy—are mostly at the mouths of the rivers that drain the upland moors and reach the sea as broad estuaries. I put rivers on my map, decided which were navigable for any distance—and *presto!* I had many places for my raiders to plunder, distant from one another, spots for Druyan to try to protect from the back of her magic-bred horse.

A primitive map has charm—perhaps one of your characters drew it—but there are tricks to convincing cartography. You can't draw a straight line without a ruler? Relax! Nobody can, and there are rather few straight lines in nature anyway. Now get yourself a real map. Any continent or bit of one will do. Put tracing paper over your selection. Pencil some outlines, imagining how the coast changes as the sea level rises—or falls. Hills become islands, islands change into peninsulas. Valleys become arms of the sea. The combination of wind and wave nibbles cliffs, isolating outcrops. It's your pick.

Change the scale. Use an island to make a continent, or vice versa. Turn your map upside down. When I designed Esdragon and Calandra, I basically used Europe—but I stood it on end, balanced on the tip of Portugal. Copy the shape of the water spot on your ceiling or the last patch of snow lingering on your sidewalk.

Study actual maps. Where do rivers flow? How do they look? Mountain ranges trap rain and alter climate. So where will your forest be? Your dry grasslands? Your band of unicorn hunters needs to cross the Dragonspike Mountains. Where are the passes? Are they open year-round or only seasonally? The threat of being trapped by an early winter can add drama. A map will remind you of that.

God, as Mies van der Rohe said, is in the details. As the creator of your paper world, you have responsibilities. *You* must concern yourself with the details, for there is no *Fodor's Guide to Middle Earth,* or Esdragon, or your elfin kingdom. Which brings us to the Rule of Names.

WHAT'S IN A NAME?

Basic rules for name use apply to all fiction. Just as you vary your sentence lengths, so you should choose names with differing lengths and sounds. Your names must not all begin with the same letter of the alphabet. Characters and countries must not be easily confused with one another. A name that brings to mind an over-the-counter remedy will not work for your hero.

World-makers need to name *everything.* Adam got off easy doing just the animals! I need to name kingdoms, heroes, continents, castles, islands, mountains, rivers, lakes, gods, horses, magic swords and cats. Unlike the author of the police procedural, I can't get my names by stabbing a random finger into the phone book.

Names in fantasy present special pleasures and certain problems. Names must always be apt, but you can toss off grand heroic names without the twinge of conscience you'd feel about giving such names to real children who'd be attending real-world schools. Remember, though, that names are tools. They make your invented world convincing and solid, but they must evoke the feel of *your* world. You can't just put the *Encyclopedia of Mythology* into a blender. In folkloric tradition, names have serious power: To know a creature's true name is to control it. That power carries over into fiction. Poorly chosen names can strain your reader's willing suspension of disbelief until it snaps. And then where are you?

You will be wise not to leave your naming to chance, or to the last minute. Under the pressure of mid-paragraph, you will either heave up a melange of x's, q's, and z's, or you'll clutch and settle for names as bland as tapioca. Planning ahead avoids both extremes. Compile a list of useful names.

You can keep that list in your PC or on the backs of old envelopes, but a small notebook is the handiest. I use an address book—durably hardbound, alphabetized pages, large enough not to be easily mislaid. I list names down the left margins, circling those I use and noting where. I may reuse a name from time to time, certain names being as common in Esdragon as John is in this world.

I glean and gather from sources readily available to all. Start with baby-name books. The older the better; you aren't after the trendy and popular. Copy whatever catches your eye. Histories of popular names offer archaic forms and less common variants. Rhisiart, in *The Wizard's Shadow,* is a name that is simply a Welsh version of Richard. The Welsh struggle to represent with their alphabet the sounds of a name they got from Norman French gives the name an exotic look.

Invent your own names. Dickens did it. Lord Dunsany was a master at it. Tolkien invented whole *languages* and took his names from them. You may enjoy playing with sounds. When I wrote *The Ring of Allaire,* I struggled for a week for a proper name for Valadan, my immortal warhorse. Wanting a proud, noble, brave name, I began with *val,* from valiant, and went on from there. Whereas Kessallia in *The Prince of Ill Luck* just popped out of my subconscious one day. Learn to spot a "keeper" like that.

Use the phone book. Use the newspaper—all those lists of engagements, weddings, obituaries. Chop off the front half of a name, or use just the ending. Stick a syllable of one name onto part of another. Minor changes yield fresh names. Switching just one letter made Robert into *Robart,* and gave Druyan's brother a familiar yet not ordinary name.

Watch movie credits. Watch the Olympics—you'll hear scads of less usual names, like Oksana, and they're *spelled* for you, right on the screen. What could be easier?

Once you have your names, use them wisely. Pick those that fit your story and its cultures. Save the rest for your next project.

The true test of imagination may be to name a cat, as Samuel Butler said. I doubt that correctly naming a dragon is far down the difficulty scale, though. World-making and myth-making are not for the faint-hearted, nor the short attention span. The good news: No license is required! Only the will to do the job right—which is the *real* power behind *any* wizard's spell.

Re-Evaluating Some Definitions of Fantasy

Edmund Little

Edmund Little is lecturer of Russian studies at the University of Hull and author of *The Fantasts*, a study of five major fantasy writers. Little first relays the suppositions of J.R.R. Tolkien and Colin Manlove regarding the definitions of fantasy, and then addresses which theories are still valid and which need to be re-evaluated. He believes that the diversity of the genre means that some of the hard and fast rules must be discarded in favor of a wider, unbiased definition.

Despite its popularity the Fantasy genre does not lend itself to easy definition. J.R.R. Tolkien is accepted as the chief Fantast of our age and his name is often linked with certain other, highly diverse writers, who are also rated as authors of Fantasy. Among them are Mervyn Peake (1911–1968) who became a 'cult' figure soon after Tolkien; Charles Williams (1886–1945) who was a friend of Tolkien and of C.S. Lewis (1898–1963), another highly acclaimed Fantast; George Macdonald (1824–1905) who allegedly influenced Williams, Tolkien and Lewis; William Morris (1834–1896) and Lord Dunsany (1878–1957). It would be difficult to deduce a coherent, consistent definition of the Fantasy genre from these writers who differ so markedly from one another in content, style and register. E.F. Bleiler, in a complaint echoed by C.N. Manlove several years later, affirmed that Fantasy may be all things to all men, and professed himself at a loss to answer what is meant by the term. Obviously Fantasy implies a literature which is non-realistic, but there is plenty of non-realistic literature which, in popular critical writing, does not seem to be considered Fantasy. Bram Stoker (1847–1912), author of Dracula (1897) is rarely numbered among the Fantasts, and nor, apparently, is Kafka (1883–1924).

IN RESPONSE TO TOLKIEN

The two best and most coherent attempts to bring some order in the situation are by Tolkien himself in his essay on fairy stories, and by C.N. Manlove in his important study of Modern Fantasy. Tolkien's remarks are much quoted and, in view of his own eminence as a Fantast, deserve particular attention. He views the Fantast as the subcreator of a Secondary World, an 'other' world, which stands in contrast to Primary existence. Tolkien avoids the term 'real', world. Inside the Secondary World, what the author relates is 'true', and should inspire Secondary Belief in the reader. Tolkien strongly emphasises the need for inner consistency. Anybody, he asserts, can say 'the green sun'. To create a Secondary World inside which that green sun becomes credible requires special narrative skill. He makes the important proviso that, should any satire be present, the magic itself must never be made fun of, but must be taken seriously, neither laughed at nor explained away. He concludes with an impassioned discourse on the purpose of fairy stories which he sees as 'recovery', 'escape' and 'consolation'. They enable us to recover a clearer vision of the world '. . . so that the things seen clearly may be freed from the drab blur of triteness or familiarity. . . .' They provide escape from a world which has grown industrialised or dull, and finally an escape from death. Consolation is provided by the happy ending which, Tolkien asserts, all complete fairy stories must have.

Tolkien's statements were written with his own work in mind. They cannot be applied consistently to all works popularly assigned to the Fantasy genre. Many offer no recovery or consolation, and a reader might wish to escape *from* rather than into them. The happy ending is not a descriptive feature of many worlds and can hardly be made prescriptive. There is no joy in Peake's Gormenghast, and none in Lord Dunsany's Pegana. Magic need not be treated in totally humourless fashion. Merlyn in T.H. White's Arthurian novel is presented as a comic figure whose magic can go wrong, but that is not a satisfactory reason for excluding the work from Fantasy. Inhabitants of Faërie need not be infallible or humourless, as Tolkien's own work shows, and there is no reason why a wizard should not make a mistake in his spells.

Even Gandalf comes close to absurdity when he fails (despite being a learned loremaster) to identify the simple password which will open the door to the mines of Moria.

TOLKIEN'S VIEWS APPLY TO ALL LITERATURE

Secondary Worlds can have marvels without having magic, and fairy stories need not necessarily contain fairies, as Tolkien himself observes. Tolkien therefore has not defined either fairy stories or Fantasy as such. Instead he has defined the task faced by *any* writer of creative fiction, because, in a sense, all creative fiction is Fantasy. The life and people of the Primary World supply the imagination of the writer with raw material. The finished product in the shape of a novel, story or play might be realistic to the mind's eye, and command the Secondary Belief of enthralled readers; but it still remains a Secondary World, the verity of which is open to doubt. A student, who was once asked to read some novels famous for their psychological and social realism, made the querulous complaint that they were as unrealistic as anything else he had been obliged to read in that they lacked any explicit reference to sex or sanitation. A less perverse reproach may be levelled at the European Romantics who sang the joys of nature, outdoor life and oriental climates without mentioning illness, insects and other disadvantages attached to these states.

Life always has to be pruned and tidied up before it can enter literature, and few works reflect the Primary World in a pure, undistorted image. A truly realistic novel would be the literary equivalent of the map in Lewis Carroll's *Sylvie and Bruno Concluded* which aims to be as large as the country it represents. Like any other artist, therefore, a writer has to be selective, choosing his characters from life or from his own imagination, placing them in a setting and putting them into action. He can clarify or obscure their motivations, inject his own judgments into the work, or maintain a pose of detached objectivity—if it is possible to be objective about characters one has invented and placed in situations of one's own contriving. Outright changes in the Primary World are permitted. Few novels or plays reproduce human speech with all its padding words, repetitions, pauses and grunts. Phonetic renderings of local dialect can strain the eyes and ears of all but the most fervent realist, as D.H. Lawrence proved by reproducing the *patois* of Mellors in *Lady Chatterley's Lover.* Shakespeare's plays embellish reality by having people speak in iambic pentameters and blank verse. When Cleopatra informs Antony that 'eternity was on our lips and eyes . . .' she is speaking great poetry, but few inhabitants of the Primary World could express their love so eloquently.

Consistency is a virtue Tolkien professes to see in tales about Faërie, but its presence in realistic literature can hardly be taken for granted. Authors of high repute have permitted situational and psychological absurdities which could not occur in the Primary World. Oscar Wilde's play *The Importance of Being Earnest* is securely founded on them. Even the impeccable Jane Austen has implausibilities of a less extravagant kind. Miss Morland of *Northanger Abbey* is foolish enough to see life through the eyes of Mrs. Radcliffe and her Gothic novels, but she is not made quite foolish enough to be plausibly taken in by the hypocritical Isabella for so long. Sir Thomas Bertram of *Mansfield Park* is a perspicacious, intelligent man, but only towards the novel's end does he become aware of Mrs. Norris's blatant malice and stupidity. Mr. Palmer of *Sense and Sensibility* undergoes a radical, inexplicable character change from nastiness to affability. Such points are minor compared to the wild coincidences in Dostoyevsky's novels or the liberties taken with plot and psychology by authors of detective and thriller fiction.

Tolkien's Exclusions

Tolkien attempts to set limits around Faërie by excluding from it certain types of writing. He discounts such works as *Gulliver's Travels*—not on account of its satirical intent:

> I rule it out, because the vehicle of the satire, brilliant invention though it may be, belongs to the class of travellers' tales. Such tales report many marvels, but they are marvels to be seen in this mortal world in some region of our own time and space; distance alone conceals them.

This seems a minor quibble. Gulliver travels in the Primary World or, to be more exact, in Swift's replica of it, and visits distant countries. Is this much different in principle from Tolkien's Middle-earth which is set in the far history of our Primary World? Why should distance in space be less worthy than distance in time? Moreover, *The Hobbit* and *The Lord of the Rings* are travellers' tales. Bilbo and Frodo make great journeys 'there and back again', both of which have been recorded in 'The Red Book of Westmarch', the manuscript source from which Tolkien claims to have drawn both tales.

Tolkien also excludes any story which uses the machinery of dream, the dreaming of actual human sleep, to explain the apparent occurrence of marvels. A fairy story, he thinks, should be presented as 'true', and it cannot therefore tolerate any mechanism which suggests it to be a figment or an illusion. Because of their dream framework Lewis Carroll's Alice stories cannot be accepted as fairy stories. The very root of their marvels, Tolkien adds, is satiric, a mockery of unreason. The dream element is not a mere machinery of introduction and ending, but inherent in the action and transitions.

Tolkien raises several interesting questions which should be explored further. The Alice worlds are presented within a technical dream framework, but Tolkien does not pursue the question of what actually makes them *dream-like*, and does it follow, in any case, that a dream is 'untrue'? Whether Alice's adventures can be reckoned a dream is itself a debatable point, and having made no objection to the satire inherent in *Gulliver's Travels,* why object to its presence in the Alice books?

Another type of story excluded from Faërie is the beast-fable:

> The magical understanding by men of the proper languages of birds and beasts and trees, that is much nearer to the true purposes of Faërie. But in stories in which no human being is concerned; or in which the animals are the heroes and heroines, and men and women, if they appear, are mere adjuncts; and above all those in which the animal form is only a mask upon a human face, a device of the satirist or preacher, in these we have beast-fable and not fairy-story. . .

There are several objections to this. The very possession of language by beasts and trees is, in itself a humanising factor, particularly if they can hold rational conversations of the sort we associate with the human species. And why can animals not be the centre of a story? Tolkien writes before the appearance of Richard Adams' novel *Watership Down* which places rabbits at the centre of attention. Admittedly a crudely moralistic beast-fable would kill the charm of a work, just as a too blatant 'message' can kill most works of creative fiction, but *Watership Down* has no crude message of this kind. Among beast-fables Tolkien numbers Kenneth Grahame's *The Wind in the Willows,* a work not immediately known for blatant preaching or satire, but, even if a work does have satirical elements, much depends upon the reader's ability to perceive them. *Gulliver's Travels* has been read by many children and adults who have been oblivious to its satirical purpose, whereas Tolkien, who denied all satirical and allegorical intent, saw his *The Lord of the Rings* interpreted in such terms. What matters, after all, is whether a work can stand up on its own after the object of the satire or allegory has been forgotten. Such is the case with Swift's work but not, unfortunately, with the work of Tolkien's fellow Fantasy writer, C.S. Lewis, in whose books christian allegory is so obvious that, if Tolkien's doctrine were followed, they should lose their place in Faërie.

In Response to Manlove

Manlove formulates the following succinct and useful definition of Fantasy:

> A fiction evoking wonder and containing a substantial and irreducible element of supernatural or impossible worlds, beings or objects with which the reader or the characters within the story become on at least partly familiar terms.

A work must be an acknowledged piece of fiction by its author, and not an account of remarkable experiences which he claims to be true. As an example of the latter, Manlove cites Bishop Leadbeater's account of fairies in Ireland. The point is a good one, but the example unfortunate. Leadbeater was not attempting to tell a tale. Whatever the authenticity of his vision, he was recording his observations of the fairy population. His work has no plot or story line. An anthropologist, writing up his observations of life in primitive tribes, would not be regarded as an author of realistic fiction, so there is no reason to regard the bishop as an author of fantastic fiction in the literary sense. It is a work such as Joan Grant's *Winged Pharaoh* which causes problems of classification. Set in the first dynasty of ancient Egypt, and narrated in the first person, it tells of a young princess who enters a temple to be trained as a priest of Anubis, thereby acquiring supernatural powers. She afterwards rules as joint Pharaoh with her brother. The novel fulfils all the requirements of the above definition, and could therefore be rated a first class novel in the Fantasy genre. Matters are complicated, however, because the 'novel' is allegedly an autobiography of one of Joan Grant's many previous incarnations. She believes it to be true in Primary, not Secondary World terms. A definition of the novel's genre will therefore depend upon an assessment of Joan Grant's truthfulness or sanity, which readers cannot judge anyway. And, if the novel can be enjoyed as Fantasy, does it matter what its author believes?

Lin Carter seems to think it does. She states with alarming certainty that the poets of the Homeric age believed in their gods and monsters. So to a lesser extent, did the authors of medieval romances. None of them, therefore, was consciously writing Fantasy. William Morris, on the other hand, was an educated Englishman who knew that dragons were a biological impossibility but still put them into a story. This point of view bristles with difficulties. In many cases it is impossible to assess the author's own beliefs, and why should a reader be bound to them? For Dante, who believed in heaven purgatory and hell, his *Divine Comedy* was presumably a work of creative fiction. A reader, who considers angels and devils to be in the same category of impossible beings as elves and unicorns, might prefer to see it as Fantasy.

UNTENABLE DISTINCTIONS

Manlove draws an interesting distinction between Fantasy and Science Fiction:

> Peake's Gormenghast, for instance, has no connection with our sphere of possibility: the author suggests no way in which it might be reached from our world, nor does he give it any location in time or space. Nothing 'supernatural' or magical by our standards is in fact present. . . . Only the existence of the realm itself is impossible or wholly 'other' in relation to ours. . . . In science fiction we find that such otherness is never present, however remote the location: for example, the planets described in Frank Herbert's *Dune* or the far galaxy in Asimov's *Foundation* trilogy are possible worlds in that they are set in our universe and describe the sorts of events and civilizations that conceivably could exist, whether now or in the future.

A distinction between Fantasy and Science Fiction based on conceivability is difficult to sustain. Gormenghast is not located in a place or time one can readily identify, but that alone does not make it an 'other' world. Although a bizarre place, packed with ludicrous people, it is less strange than many worlds presented in Science Fiction. If a world becomes possible merely because its author pronounces it to be on another planet, then Peake would only need to insert a statement to that effect and his Gormenghast would become, in theory, a 'possible' world.

The *Foundation* trilogy has itself many inconceivable and impossible things: jumps by space ship through 'hyper-space', atomic reactors the size of walnuts, and men with startling powers of mental telepathy. The 'time kettles' of another Asimov novel, and the time 'shuttle' of Poul Anderson's short stories, are no more conceivable in Primary World terms than the magic stone of Charles Williams' novel, or the magic rings by which C.S. Lewis sends children into other dimensions. Neither rings nor the dimensions are less conceivable than the 'parallel' universes of another Asimov novel. When Faërie is industrialised and given a technology, it is called Science Fiction. The machine replaces magic, technical jargon the spell or incantation, and the wizard acquires a labcoat to be called a scientist. Different types of magic, perhaps, but both are equally impossible.

Manlove follows Tolkien in asserting that the supernatural or impossible element in a story must be substantial or irreducible, and therefore rejects beast-fables, and the Alice books: the former because the supernatural is part of the moral purpose of the tale, the latter because the supernatural is a symbolic extension of a purely human mind. T. H. White's *The Once and Future King* is excluded because Arthur, Merlyn and Gramarye 'are all versions of Britain idealized'.

The final clause in Manlove's definition states that the mortal characters in a story should be on at least partly familiar terms with the supernatural or impossible elements within it. This distinguishes Fantasy from the ghost or horror story, where the supernatural is encountered as an alien force, particularly effective when it intrudes into ordinary domestic life. Supernatural forces are present in Fantasy too, but they are matched by almost equally potent supernatural powers for good. This too is an interesting distinction which loses its force on closer inspection. Bram Stoker's *Dracula* represents an intrusion of evil into the domestic affairs of a group of people, and he is matched by potent powers for good in the shape of brave young men and sacred symbols. The characters in the work, and the readers, become far more familiar with the Count than anybody ever does with Tolkien's Sauron, and yet the novel is not generally numbered among works of Fantasy. Moreover, supernatural interventions need not always be gruesome. They can be friendly and helpful. Whether hostile or cooperative, the intrusion of supernatural forces into human life is impossible by normal Primary World standards, and the separation of ghost and horror stories from Fantasy on these grounds is unconvincing.

A definition of Fantasy to include all the works commonly accepted as belonging to the genre would be a near impossible achievement. Rather than quibble ungratefully over other people's attempts, it would be more constructive to return to the concept which both Tolkien and Manlove see as the essence of Faërie and Fantasy: the making of a Secondary World which is 'other' and 'impossible'. All writers of creative fiction are subcreators of Secondary Worlds. The Secondary World of a non-fantastic writer will be as close to the Primary World as his talents and the needs of his art will allow. By the very nature of his art, some changes have to be made to the Primary World before it enters literature, if only to make the work easier to read. A licence is granted to writers of 'normal' creative fiction to change the Primary World for the purpose of their art. Fantasy begins when an author's Secondary World goes beyond that licence and becomes 'other'. It is impossible to seek a definition of Fantasy without enquiring about the licence and its limits. Which aspects of 'Reality' have to be changed, and to what degree, to turn the normal Secondary World of creative fiction into an 'other' world of Fantasy? Answers to these questions require an examination of some Secondary Worlds, but a few general observations can be made now.

JUDGING THE "OTHERNESS" OF SECONDARY WORLDS

Whatever the state of affairs inside a Secondary World, a degree of 'otherness' can be imparted by that world's location in relation to the Primary World. Some works of Fantasy do not take the reader into a Secondary World away from our own. Instead, the author constructs a replica of the Primary World into which he introduces impossible creatures or objects, or allows impossible things to happen. Bram Stoker introduces a vampire into Victorian London, and Alan Garner a unicorn into Manchester. In this type of narrative the reader enjoys a certain security, because he still has his feet on Primary soil, no matter how pleasant or repelling the intruding forces might be. The result is perhaps less exotic, less glamorous than the subcreation of a new 'other' world away from Primary life, which might explain a general reluctance to accept such Secondary Worlds as Fantastic, demonstrated by Tolkien's rejection of *Gulliver's Travels* and Manlove's desire to put ghost stories into a separate genre. Why the intrusion of impossible objects, like magic stones, should bring Charles Williams into Fantasy, whereas the intervention of equally impossible creatures such as ghosts, or vampires, should put a work into a different genre is a little hard to see.

The second type of location is more readily admitted to Fantasy. A Secondary World is set apart and made distinct from the Primary World, and yet still remains in some sort of visible relationship with it. If previous terms are adhered to, such a subcreation should be called a *Tertiary World*, because the author's replica of the Primary World is, strictly speaking, itself a Secondary World. A Tertiary World can be set apart from our own in time, and placed in the past or future of our own world. It can be distanced in space, and located in some region of our own planet *(The Water Babies; Gulliver's Travels)*. It may be located on some other planet of our Primary Universe. A popular device is to locate the Tertiary World in another 'dimension', which is reached through some type of doorway or by some means of transport. The children of Alan Garner's *Elidor* reach the country of that name on the vibrations of a fiddle played within the ruins of a church. C.S. Lewis' children find their way into Narnia through the back of a wardrobe. His adult hero Ransom reached Perelandra in a mysterious box. A more controversial means of entering another dimension, condemned by Tolkien, is the dream.

There are many possible permutations. If a Tertiary World is reached by some form of machinery, such as a space ship, or if the World possesses a technology of its own, the work will probably be labelled Science Fiction. If reached by machine-less methods, by spell or magic doors or magic rings, it will be dubbed Fantasy. The same principle, however, operates in each case: a world set apart from our own is entered through a type of doorway or by some form of transport.

A third type of location is a world set apart from the Primary World but having no visible link with it. The works mentioned above have a traveller or a dreamer who leaves the Primary World for adventures in Secondary life. In the third category Secondary Worlds are simply presented as existing, and there are no intermediary characters to travel between them and Primary existence. There is no clue as to the whereabouts of Lord Dunsany's Pegana. The world might be in the past, present or future of this or some other planet or dimension. The very absence of a link can have an unsettling effect on the reader, quite apart from any strange things to be found within the world itself.

Theoretically it would be possible for an author to place his Secondary World in another dimension, or on another planet, and then to narrate a tale of suburban life in a modern English provincial town. The 'otherness' of such a tale would lie in the intriguing assumption that life in other dimensions could be an exact replica of the more humdrum kinds of existence available here. As amusing as the assumption is, it is not the sort of Secondary World lovers of Fantasy would wish to see. Location plays an important role in determining a degree of 'otherness', but works commonly accepted as Fantastic also contain 'marvels'. The Primary World has not only to be duplicated, even in another dimension. It has to be changed.

Fantasy Books for Adolescents Inspire and Empower

Tamora Pierce

Tamora Pierce, the author of several young adult fantasy novels, believes that adolescents respond to the idealism and imagination in fantasy, and that the genre inspires and empowers them with hope and optimism. By examining numerous popular books for young adults, she concluded that well-drawn heroes and villains can give young readers the strength to stand up to the adversities in their own lives.

I wonder why readers choose to read fantasy; rather, I wonder why more of them *don't*. Until they reach school age, children are offered little else on almost a continuous basis. The groundwork for a love of the fanciful is laid by children's literature, from A.A. Milne to Dr. Seuss, and from Curious George to Max and his Wild Things.

Once children enter school, however, emphasis shifts from imaginative to reality-based writing, and many youngsters grow away from speculative fiction—but not all. Those who stay with it do so for many reasons, and it comes to fill a number of needs in their lives.

STIMULATING YOUNG MINDS

One of the things I have learned about YAs [young adults] is that they respond to the idealism and imagination they find in everything they read. They haven't spent years butting their heads against brick walls; the edge of their enthusiasm, and of their minds, is still sharp. Some of the most perceptive social and political commentary I've heard in the last eight years or so has come from my readers. Young people have the time and emotional energy to devote to causes, unlike so many of us, losing our revolutionary (or evolutionary) drive as we spend ourselves on the details and chores that fill adult life. They take up causes, from the environment, to human disaster relief, to politics. We encourage them, and so we should: there is a tremendous need for those who feel passionately and are willing to work at what they care about, whatever their cause may be. YAs are also dreamers; this is expected and, to a degree, encouraged as they plan for the future. Their minds are flexible, recognizing few limits. Here the seeds are sown for the great visions, those that will change the future for us all. We give our charges goals, heroes whose feats they can emulate, and knowledge of the past, but they also need fuel to spark and refine ideas, the same kind of fuel that fires idealism.

That fuel can be found—according to the writings of [psychologists] Jung, Bettelheim, M. Ester Harding, and Joseph Campbell—in the mighty symbols of myth, fairy tales, dreams, legends—and fantasy. Haven't we felt their power? Remember that flush of energy and eagerness we felt as Arthur drew the sword from the stone? It's the same as that which bloomed the first time—or even the fifth or sixth time—we heard Dr. King say "I have a dream." An eyedropper's worth of that energy can feed days of activity, hard and sometimes dirty work, fund-raising, letter writing. It can ease an idealist over small and big defeats.

Here is where fantasy, in its flesh and modern (i.e. post-1900) forms, using contemporary sensibilities and characters youngsters identify with, reigns supreme. Here the symbols of meaningful struggle and of truth as an inner constant exist in their most undiluted form outside myth and fairy tale: Tolkein's forces of Light fighting a mind-numbing Darkness; Elizabeth Moon's lone paladin facing pain and despair with only faith to sustain her (in *Oath of Gold*, 1989); Diane Duane's small choir of deep sea creatures holding off the power of death and entropy at the risk of the world's life and their own (*Deep Wizardry*, 1985). These stories appear to have little to do with reality, but they do provide readers with the impetus to challenge the way things are, something YAs respond to wholeheartedly. Young people are drawn to battles for a discernable higher good; the images of such battles evoke their passion. (I would like to note here that some of the writers mentioned herein normally are considered to be adult writers. Fantasy, even more than other genres, has a large crossover audience, with YAs raiding the adult shelves once they deplete their part of the store or library, and adults slipping into the youth sections.)

A LITERATURE OF POSSIBILITIES

Fantasy, along with science fiction, is a literature of *possibilities*. It opens the door to the realm of "What If," challenging readers to see beyond the concrete universe and to envision other ways of living and alternative mindsets. Everything in speculative universes, and by association the real world, is mutable. Intelligent readers will come to relate the questions raised in these books to their own lives. If a question nags at youngsters intensely enough, they will grow up to devise an answer—to move their world forward, because ardent souls can't stand an unanswered question.

The question of a place to belong is a burning issue in all YA literature, not just the speculative variety. Fantasy writers seem to have an affinity for it, particularly for the variation of outsiders who find, or rather *make*, a place that is their own. It is obvious in Mercedes Lackey's "Arrows" series (DAW), in which the young heroine flees an abusive home to create a niche for a small, scared girl-child among the legendary Heralds. It is central to Barbara Hambly's books, from her "Darwath" trilogy (1982) to her recent *Dog Wizard* (1993). A personal niche is the series-long quest of Lloyd Alexander's hero Taran ("Prydain Chronicles") and the drive that moves Schmendrick, the mage of Peter Beagle's *The Last Unicorn* (1987). Next to the normal, human flaws of my protagonists, the creation of a unique place in the world is the thing my readers mention most often in their letters. Some youngsters will always say, "But that only happens in *books*," but fantasy readers seem to know that what happens in books can be carried over, that the idea of change is universal, and that willpower and work are formidable forces, wherever they are applied.

FANTASY EMPOWERS

Fantasy, more than any other genre, is a literature of empowerment. In the real world, kids have little say. This is a given; it is the nature of childhood. In fantasy, however short, fat, unbeautiful, weak, dreamy, or unlearned individuals may be, they find a realm in which those things are negated by strength. The catch—there is *always* a catch—is that empowerment brings trials. Good novels in this genre never revolve around heroes who, once they receive the "Spatula of Power," call the rains to fill dry wells, end all war, and clear up all acne. Heroes and heroines contend as much with their granted wishes as readers do in normal life. Anne McCaffrey's Menolly, heroine of *Dragonsinger* (1977), discovers life at Harper Hall isn't all music, as she'd dreamed, but hard work and entanglement in human problems and politics. In Edgar Eager's *Half Magic* (1954), children receive a wishing coin that does things only by halves, a truly mixed blessing with which each of them has to cope. While Bruce Coville's "Magic Shop" series customers may not wish for a ring that changes the wearer to a werewolf, a dragon's egg that hatches, or a talking toad, they get them—and have to solve the many problems created by such possessions. Young readers seem to come away from the char-

---

IN DEFENSE OF FANTASY: LEARNING TO FIGHT THE DRAGONS

As the guest of honor at the Booksellers Association Conference in April 1993, fantasy author Terry Pratchett spoke about the importance of fantasy to a child's development.

Why does the third of the three brothers, who shares his food with the old woman in the wood, go on to become king of the country? Why does James Bond manage to disarm the nuclear bomb a few seconds before it goes off rather than, as it were, a few seconds afterwards? Because a universe where that did not happen would be a dark and hostile place. Let there be goblin hordes, let there be terrible environmental threats, let there be giant mutated slugs if you really must, but let there also be hope. It may be a grim, thin hope, an Arthurian sword at sunset, but let us know that we do not live in vain. . . .

And fantasy's readers might also learn, in the words of Stephen Sondheim, that witches can be right and giants can be good. They learn that where people stand is perhaps not as important as which way they face. This is part of the dangerous process of growing up. . . .

So let's not get frightened when the children read fantasy. It is the compost for a healthy mind. It stimulates the inquisitive nodes. It may not appear as "relevant" as books set more firmly in the child's environment, or whatever hell the writer believes to be the child's environment, but there is some evidence that a rich internal fantasy life is as good and necessary for a child as healthy soil is for a plant, for much the same reasons.

acters' mishaps not depressed but energized, as if the protagonist's struggle was something they survived as well.

One of the greatest legendary and imaginative symbols is that of the knight in shining armor. Paramedics, social workers, advocacy lawyers, (and writers) keep it in some corner of their minds, while they work in settings that in no way resemble the feudal agrarian culture from which those symbols are drawn. Combat power holds allure for many fantasy readers, and the genre presents it in every form one could desire, starting with Arthurian legend. Strength isn't measured by modern world terms but usually in medieval ones, and such strength can change the fates of people and of nations. Here also, battles aren't always won by those who are big and strong, although such heroes are a popular aspect of this kind of fiction, from Little John and Lancelot to David Eddings's militant church knights.

Combat heroes who don't fit a traditionally heroic mold exist as well. Dwarves, for example. No one laughs at a dwarf as written by Tolkein or Elizabeth Moon. They are short, squat, uncomely people who are also clever, tireless, formidable opponents. Sometimes they are heroines. Robin McKinley's Harry in *The Blue Sword* (1982) and Aerin in *The Hero and the Crown* (1984) start off as amateurs with little or no sword training. Both work hard to achieve their mastery. Harry is called to it by the powers that guard her new home and an awareness of disaster on its way; Aerin simply to make her own place in the world.

In fantasy, those normally perceived as unimportant are vital players. David Eddings's five-book "Belgariad" series, beginning with *Pawn of Prophecy*, is the tale of a boy who is caught up in world-changing events whether he wants to be or not. He walks in the company of heroes as a very junior partner and, in spite of his errors, becomes one of them, a process with which any YA can identify. In Tolkein's "Lord of the Rings" trilogy, plain, simple, everyday folk are taken into that same wider tapestry, where they affect the course of history simply by being who they are.

MAGIC AND WONDER

Most important of all in fantasy is that great equalizer between the powerful and the powerless: magic, the thing that keeps young children captivated by fairy tales and older ones enthralled by wizards, from Merlin to Zilpha Keatley

Snyder's Mr. Mazzeeck in *Black and Blue Magic* (1972). Some get both in one, as more and more authors retell the ancient stories with a modern point of view. My favorite is Robin McKinley's *Beauty* (1978). The glitter of magic lures readers into a new universe in Diana Wynne Jones's *Charmed Life* (1989), and keeps them there when Cat's relationship with his rotten sister must feel all too painfully familiar. Even magic comes with complications: good fantasy won't let its readers off the hook. YAs live the inner conflict of Diane Duane's young mage Nita in *Deep Wizardry*, who rashly promises to do whatever is needed to help the marine wizards complete their magical ceremony, only to learn she has agreed to die, and that to default on that vow will undo their work, her own work, and that of her co-mage and friend, Christopher. Snyder's Harry Houdini Marco acquires truly horrific bruises and creates even more havoc as he tries to manage a pair of wings without getting found out.

Fantasy is also important to a group that I deeply hope is small: those whose lives are so grim that they cling to everything that takes them completely away for *any* length of time. I speak of readers like I was, from families that are now called dysfunctional. While the act of reading transported me out of reality for the time it took me to read, nothing carried over into my thoughts and dreams until I discovered fantasy. I visited Tolkien's Mordor often for years, not because I *liked* what went on there, but because on that dead horizon, and then throughout the sky overhead, I could see the interplay and the lasting power of light and hope. It got me through.

Fantasy creates hope and optimism in readers. It is the pure stuff of wonder, the kind that carries over into everyday life and colors the way readers perceive things around them. I think everyone could use some extra hope and wonder as we enter a new millennium. It can be found in the children's, young adult, and science fiction and fantasy sections of bookstores and libraries everywhere.

Fantasy Allows Children to Question the Status Quo

Jeanne Murray Walker

Jeanne Murray Walker, a professor at the University of Delaware, believes that fantasy books help children to grow into independent, creative people. They guide the child through important rites of passage, and allow them to question the world around them in a healthy, confident way. She illustrates her points with examples from C.S. Lewis's *The Lion, the Witch, and the Wardrobe*, Norman Juster's *Phantom Tollbooth*, and Ursula K. Le Guin's *Wizard of Earthsea*.

Fantasy is often ridiculed for its lack of ideas, and readers of fantasy are attacked for their desire to escape. Withdrawal is not a coping strategy most thoughtful adults want to teach children. In fact, if fantasy as a form were merely a way of escaping, it might create problems for children, who need all the practice they can get dealing with a world that grows increasingly complex. But far from isolating children or encouraging them to escape from their social responsibilities, "high fantasy" unites people into groups and reinforces the values around which those groups cohere. It might be argued, in fact, that if fantasy presents any danger, it is the danger of preparing the reader for obedient, uncritical participation in a comforting, authoritarian system. But the best children's fantasies encourage questioning of commonly held cultural values rather than mere conformity to them. Ursula K. Le Guin's *Wizard of Earthsea*, C.S. Lewis's *Lion, the Witch, and the Wardrobe,* and Norman Juster's *Phantom Tollbooth*, examples of such fantasies, provide good cases to examine in detail. . . .

Excerpted from "Critical Issues and Approaches," by Jeanne Murray Walker, in *Teaching Children's Literature: Issues, Pedagogy, Resources*, edited by Glenn Edward Sadler. Copyright © 1992 by the Modern Language Association of America. Reprinted by permission of the Modern Language Association of America.

A WIZARD OF EARTHSEA AS RITE OF PASSAGE

The parallels between rites of passage and children's fantasy are evident in Le Guin's *Wizard of Earthsea*. Not only does *A Wizard* show its readers that the question of the hero's own "name," his own identity, cannot be avoided; it also indicates that his naming is an event attended by the whole society. Moreover, the naming dramatizes the old and inevitable process in which individuals define themselves in relationship to fixed positions in society. The first chapter of *A Wizard* documents the characteristics of the hero's village, analyzes the social position of wizards, describes celebrations, and illustrates the importance of the myths that perpetuate cultural memory and personal fame. This anthropological detail establishes the groundwork of assumptions and values by which the reader can interpret the behavior of the hero, Ged. But the most telling anthropological statement occurs at the conclusion of chapter 1, where Ged's rite of passage occurs.

As individuals interpret their lives through symbols and events, in their rites of passage, so Le Guin's later chapters are but dramatizations of the elements of Ged's initiation. The spring through which Ged wades is an analogue for the ocean on which he later completes his troubled quest for the shadow. The shadows that "slid and mingled" at the initiation anticipate the terrible shadow that later enters the world by Ged's hand. The new name that Ogion whispers to the boy suggests a later incident in which Ged gives the shadow the same name. The central role of Ogion at the initiation predicts his crucial role in healing the wounded sparrowhawk, the form Ged magically assumes in his flight from deadly peril. Ged's isolation during his walk through the spring prefigures his years of physical and psychological loneliness. And, of course, Ged's walking—his passage through the spring—articulates his forward movement through time and experience.

But how can a modern reader who has never gone through a rite of passage comprehend the significance of this ritual in *A Wizard of Earthsea*? It would be nonsense to argue that by experiencing this brief ritual with Ged, a reader can enjoy a status change. As we have seen, however, the work develops in great detail the elements of the rite of passage. Ged's rite of passage is an analogue to the entire plot, and the plot itself functions as a rite of passage for the reader.

Not only do the specific elements of Ged's initiation (water, a master, naming, a shadow) pattern the rest of the plot; they are used to convince the reader of the social theory that makes rites of passage meaningful. The fiction illustrates the interdependence of human beings and the social nature of individual identities, two broad assumptions that underlie rituals of passage. In fact, in its metaphor of equilibrium, *A Wizard* pushes these assumptions further to show the social aspect of all things, even nature. It portrays, too, the enforced isolation through which an initiate must pass while undergoing the change from old to new self. And it articulates forcefully the danger that threatens society in the act of initiating its members. Such themes in the novel constitute the basic social theory a reader must have in order to comprehend the context for rites of passage.

The teaching at the heart of the rite of passage, Le Guin's idea of equilibrium, challenges materialistic assumptions. Not ownership but the proper use of things gives power, Ged learns. The reader who passes through the initiation with Ged understands that "all power is one in source and end. . . . Years and distances, stars and candles, water and wind and wizardry, the craft in a man's hand and the wisdom in a tree's root: they all arise together . . . . There is no other power." To tap into that power, one must patiently master the true name and nature of everything, including oneself. Nothing could more directly contradict the quick material fix.

THE LION, THE WITCH, AND THE WARDROBE: TEACHING CHILDREN TO INTERPRET THE WORLD

In fact, *The Lion, the Witch, and the Wardrobe,* C.S. Lewis's first published Narnia story, is patterned by the same structure as that of Le Guin's work. It bears all the salient features of a rite of passage: (1) The children step from a world of ordinary social experience in London, first into the cultural sanctuary of the Professor's old house and then into the artificially defined space, time, and laws of Narnia. (2) The laws in Narnia force the children to experience and so to comprehend an interpretation of the world (value) and thus to act on it. (3) As a result of their action, they undergo a status change. (4) This status change has been prophesied since the beginning of time in Narnia: as the function of a rite of passage is to transform the initiate, so the very definition of Narnia contains the inevitability of the children's becoming adult kings and queens. (5) The wardrobe, the threshold between the ordinary world and the artificial world of Narnia, is repeatedly referred to by the narrator as a potential place of death, the potential failure of the children's status change.

As in a rite of passage, the four heroes' task is to decipher conventional symbols and internalize them. The symbols teach values and laws that govern Narnia. A familiar—indeed, overwhelmingly common Christian—interpretation of reality shapes the novel's secondary world.

Lewis calls attention in *The Lion* to the act of properly reading objects in the world. Once the children get into Narnia, they evaluate the animals and time and weather and all the events according to conventions they have learned in the past: "They're good birds in all the stories I've read. I'm sure a robin wouldn't be on the wrong side." Only Edmund refuses to generalize about values from the conventional images: "If it comes to that, which is the right side? How do we know that the fauns are in the right and the Queen (yes, I know we've been told she's a witch) is in the wrong? We don't really know anything about either."

It is worth examining why Edmund is unable to interpret conventional signs in Narnia accurately. In the first place, he has been badly educated at a "horrid school," where he started to "go wrong." As a result, Edmund has a bad temper. He snickers at people who look unusual, he teases Lucy mercilessly, he refuses to apologize when he is wrong, and he is greedy. The twin Renaissance categories, nature and nurture, are both defective in Edmund, and the defects make it impossible for him to identify the queen, when he first meets her, as a witch. Edmund accepts and eats her enchanted food. Once he has taken her magic into himself, he becomes a traitor to his brothers and sisters, informing the witch of their whereabouts. Eventually he becomes so deluded that he is unable to differentiate between a live animal and an animal that has been turned into stone by the witch.

Interpretation, like misinterpretation, is cumulative, according to *The Lion*. Therefore, as the children explore the symbols they encounter, they act, and with each act they discover more symbols to unravel. By incrementally discovering and construing symbols, the children learn, step by step, the conventional Christian interpretation of the world that lies behind the symbols of Narnia.

This interpretation, the central lore in the novel's rite of passage, repudiates materialism by associating it with the Witch. After Edmund betrays himself to the Witch in exchange for Turkish Delight, she insists that he is her property, to do with as she likes. "And so," she says, "that human creature is mine. His life is forfeit to me. His blood is my property." The system of debt and payment set up in the Dawn of Time requires that the Witch's claim on Edmund be honored. So Aslan substitutes his life for Edmund's and the Witch kills Aslan instead of Edmund. The Witch's possessive, materialistic assessment of human life is, however, finally proved wrong. As Aslan says, "though the Witch knew the Deep Magic, there is a magic deeper still which she did not know." This magic is the reversal of death.

Meaning lies behind every icon, Lewis's novel teaches, but it is possible to misunderstand *what* meaning. The many polemics and symbols, the collision of slogans and voices that compete for attention as the truth—these are mere appearances of value. If properly read, each can be understood as good or evil according to a master value system, the Christian message. It is possible to read both the book of nature and the book of culture without making the sort of mistakes Edmund does, if the reader has a willing heart and is ready to learn. Lewis's voice in the novel is that of an initiator, and the reader is the initiate. *The Lion, the Witch, and the Wardrobe* is Lewis's attempt to give the reader a good, if brief, education.

THE PHANTOM TOLLBOOTH: DIDACTICISM AND FASCISM IN FANTASY

Fantasy attempts to convince, and the voices that tell the stories in fantasy novels are initiator figures, overtly present and omniscient, solemnly counseling the reader through the images of the narrative. As we have seen, fantasy instructs its readers in the norms and truths of an identifiable social community. It portrays those truths as the standard by which adulthood is measured. And adulthood is the valued goal; unlike some other kinds of fiction, fantasy does not pretend to present a snapshot of the world that is value-neutral. Far from it. To read fantasy is to be confronted by the fact that if we, the readers of the book, cannot be shaped into adults with the hero, in some sense we will die. In fantasy, death or assent are the two choices.

It is not surprising, perhaps, that a society increasingly

more pluralistic in its values should enthusiastically clasp this didactic genre to its bosom. Crude forms of fantasy are everywhere—Dungeons and Dragons games, slick movies, the Strategic Defense Initiative (Star Wars). In all of them the good hero navigates the dangerous passage at great risk and wins. Good wins. What does that mean? In most popular fantasies, good is nothing more than us, our group, people who dress like us and eat what we eat. Fragmented as American culture is into groups—women, blacks, Jews, the poor, the elderly—with which individuals identify or are categorized by others, the nation appears to need generically good heroes as role models or symbols. Good equals us equals the successful questor. This formulation powerfully urges readers to conform; any reader who dissents dies, either as the unsuccessful questor or as the evil enemy. Fantasy in these popular versions is like a mindless police officer herding everyone into the same parking lot, shooting the resisters and stragglers.

Not all fantasy is so fascistic, of course. The best fantasy, novels like *A Wizard of Earthsea* and *The Lion, the Witch, and the Wardrobe,* presents complex and clearly defined values, not vacant symbols of the powerful versus the powerless. But even among these complex and thoughtful fantasies, *The Phantom Tollbooth* is remarkable because it examines the policelike qualities of its own form. *The Phantom Tollbooth,* like other children's fantasies, is structured as a rite of passage. Like an initiate, Milo, the child hero, steps from his habitual world into a tollbooth, which takes him to an artificially defined space and time, described as a "destination in mind," betwixt and between childhood and adulthood. This world is populated by witches, damsels, dragons, and other iconic characters. The oddity of these images makes Milo think for the first time about why he is bored and slothful in his routine school and home life. He begins to see reading and arithmetic and logic as heroic tasks. As a result he volunteers to penetrate the menacing Mountains of Ignorance so he can rescue the princesses, Rhyme and Reason, and return them to the Land of Wisdom. During his lonely, terrifying quest, he is transformed into a hero, which is to say that he has learned the value of education. And through his heroism, the social order is transformed into a place where mathematics and language return to their proper functions.

This is as didactic as anything in Lewis's fantasy; but unlike the solemn narrators in *A Wizard of Earthsea* and *The Lion, the Witch, and the Wardrobe*, the narrator of *The Phantom Tollbooth* speaks a good deal of nonsense. In the middle of a passage about the evils of loquacity, for example, Milo asks the Duke how a small wooden wagon that has no motor can be made to move. The Duke replies, "Be very quiet . . . for it goes without saying." What is the reader to make of this and the other wordplay in *The Phantom Tollbooth?*

The reader should recognize that the story emerges out of the narrator's struggle with the rules of language and genre. The legitimate rules are represented by the witch, Faintly Macabre. "For years and years" she was the Which "in charge of choosing which words were to be used for all occasions." Confined to a dungeon when Rhyme and Reason were banished, she bides her time, eating sugar-coated punctuation, while the language of Dictionapolis languishes in disorder. Punctuation should order sentences. The prescriptive and conventional forms of language and literary genres should not be locked up; they are necessary to make meaning. Therefore, the Which must be released before Milo can quest.

But if some forms of linguistic didacticism are kin to the questing mind ("You can call me Aunt Faintly"), others are arbitrary and bullying. Officer Short Shrift arrests Milo for spilling a cartload of letters. Shrift throws into Milo's indictment the additional crimes of forgetting his birthday, "having a dog with an unauthorized alarm" (a watch dog), "sowing confusion, upsetting the applecart, wreaking havoc, and mincing words." After arresting and indicting Milo, Officer Shrift turns into the judge and sentences Milo to the dungeon for six million years. Then, becoming a jailer, he locks the poor hero up. Short Shrift is discipline out of control. He is a parody of romance as police action.

To put it another way, part of the subject of *The Phantom Tollbooth* is the way words and syntax and literary genre tyrannize the reader (and presumably the writer) of romance. This fantasy turns the seams out and lets the reader look at the construction of the document itself and, by analogy, other fantasies. It shows what happens when quick and facile uses of form (Short Shrift) get the upper hand. The hero can't move. That is, the hero can't really work through questions about values, and he can't make any progress toward joining a group of adults who behave according to a clearly articulated set of values.

Even more interesting, *The Phantom Tollbooth* shows why forms like fantasy are often used mindlessly or, it may be, intentionally by people who want to dominate a readership hungry for social cohesion. Fantasy helps to order a chaotic world. And even at the level of language, chaos is everywhere. In the first place, a whole cartload of letters lies spilled nonsensically on the sidewalk. In the second place, the narrator can barely discipline the idioms of language well enough to keep the narration following a linear track of reasonable cause and effect ("it goes without saying"). Perversions of logic are everywhere ("watch dog"). And, in general, the world is full of people who are "sowing confusion," et cetera. Into this wealth of confusion a policeman wades to tidy up.

The authority of the policeman derives from his ability to absolve people of the guilt they feel for acting chaotically in a chaotic world. His name means to shrive, or to confess. Officer Shrift is presumably able to listen to confessions, assess guilt or innocence, pronounce sentences, and so clarify social issues. The problem is, he is power-mad, and, therefore, can't make distinctions. He fails to distinguish between guilt and innocence: the Humbug and the Spelling Bee, not Milo, were the ones who spilled the cartload of letters. And he fails to distinguish between the separate actions of policing, judging, and jailing. As a result, he throws out the hero with the mess. *The Phantom Tollbooth* shows that, like Officer Shrift, fantasy can shut up the voices of pluralism and throw in jail everything that doesn't conform. But the better way—the real way of enforcing social order—is Aunt Faintly's way, delicate, tactful, imaginative, and slow.

How can children avoid the tedium of shallow materialism and the cynical need to be entertained? How can they grow into an active and durable adult generation? These are the questions *The Phantom Tollbooth* asks. Humanistic education is the answer—reading, writing, arithmetic, logic— the tremendous quest children must make by themselves to cross the Mountains of Ignorance, bringing back Rhyme and Reason to Wisdom. The novel convinces us of the value of education through a nuanced and complex use of fantasy. Being convinced, we are no longer bored and self-indulgent children who fail to see why these endeavors are necessary.

We become communicants of the orthodoxy of humanism.

There may be no way of counteracting the fragmentation that bewilders American society or the materialism that makes its children passive—no way short of police action, which is worse than pluralism itself. Fantasy can't unify society, even though each of the best fantasies for children presents a single value that claims to be the key to adulthood. Fantasy longs for order; it drives toward unity. But finally, as *The Phantom Tollbooth* shows, too much order can bring everything to a halt. It is best to put up with a limited system of order, one that grows out of insight and educated choice. And as for the inevitable remaining disorder, it can be seen as plenitude gone mad. *The Phantom Tollbooth* recommends that it be viewed with affectionate hilarity.

FANTASY CANNOT REPLACE LIFE EXPERIENCES

Deprived of public rites of passage, American children nevertheless are able to substitute the rites of passage embedded in texts. But fantasy is still less effective than true rites of passage. That is partly because different fantasies proclaim different values. The deep fragmentation of American society can be only healed temporarily, that is, while the reader is undergoing the quest described in any given fantasy. But more important, fantasy fails to initiate children because the contractual agreement between the narrator-initiator and the reader-initiate is only a tacit social contract rather than an explicit one, as in rites of passage. The mark of the society is present not in the physical presence of the attending tribal members but in the conventions of the genre, fantasy. Fantasy represents society as an abstract concept; the conventions of reading are abstract. Young readers who depend on fantasy for rites of passage have no tangible community to support their transformation. Nevertheless, fantasy is valuable. It reminds young readers that there are conventions, that there is a society that can arrive at agreements, that even in their anomalous social position, they participate in social forms.

CHAPTER 2

Exploring Themes and Conventions

 Fantasy

An Integral Sense of Wonder

William Senior

William Senior, a professor at Broward Community College, undertook a unique study of the concept of wonder in fantasy. According to Senior, the best kinds of fantasy books exhibit both external and internal wonder. In other words, the sense of awe is projected both at the character in the book, and at the reader. To achieve this, the author needs to display wonder through all aspects of the book—the setting, characters, etc.—in order for the reader to believe in the imaginary creation.

At the end of the second book of *The Lord of the Rings*, Sam and Frodo have been captured by Faramir as he is setting an ambush for the Men of Harad who are marching into Mordor. Detained until the battle is over and Faramir can judge what to do with them, the hobbits wait with their two guards until the fight actually comes to them after the Southrons are routed and try to escape. Amid the confusion, noise, and horror of this encounter, one particular revelation makes Sam forget the rest: the oliphaunt. "To his astonishment and terror, and lasting delight, Sam saw a vast shape crash out of the trees and come careening down the slope. Big as a house, much bigger than a house, it looked to him, a grey-clad moving hill. Fear and wonder, maybe, enlarged him in the hobbit's eyes but the Mumak of Harad was indeed a beast of vast bulk and the like of him does not now walk in Middle Earth."

In this brief scene, Dickensian humor meets a Burkean sublime to produce Manlovian wonder. Yet the importance of this incident lies in the fact that the wonder is projected inward, at Sam, not at us as readers. It is this question of internal wonder—of the awe, surprise, amazement, fascination, experienced and expressed by and at those in fantasy

Excerpted from "Oliphaunts in the Perilous Realm: The Function of Internal Wonder in Fantasy," by William Senior, in *Functions of the Fantastic: Selected Essays from the Thirteenth International Conference on the Fantastic in the Arts*, edited by Joe Sanders. Copyright © 1995 by Joe Sanders. Reproduced with permission from Greenwood Publishing Group, Inc., Westport, CT.

fiction—that I wish to explore, for it seems to me significant and important in the construction of the secondary world of fantasy and in its effect on the reader. Effective fantasies, I will venture, rely on a combination of both outward- and inward-directed wonder to create a balance between secondary and primary worlds.

The anatomy of wonder has a long and distinguished history in the study of fantasy. Colin Manlove builds his definition from the cornerstone of wonder, citing it as the first criterion before even that of the impossible or the "cannot happen": "a fiction evoking wonder and containing a substantial and irreducible element of the supernatural." Tolkien stresses the evocation of wonder as one of the operating principles of fantasy in connecting the primary and secondary worlds and thus involving the reader's perceptions: "And actually fairy-stories deal largely, or (the better ones) mainly, with simple or fundamental things, untouched by Fantasy, but these simplicities are made all the more luminous by their setting. . . . It was in fairy-stories that I first divined the potency of words, and the wonder of things, such as stone, and wood, and iron; tree and grass; house and fire; bread and wine." Brian Attebery paraphrases the concept of estrangement in commenting that "[t]he most important thing they [fantasies] share is the sense of wonder. . . . Fantasy invokes wonder by making the impossible seem familiar and the familiar new and strange." Eric Rabkin observes that two central elements in the establishment of the fantastic are surprise and astonishment, kissing cousins to wonder, while W.R. Irwin goes so far as to state that the purpose of fantasy is to incite wonder. Others, of course, follow suit, but one thing all have in common is that they focus primarily on the external evocation of wonder, that experienced by the reader. Yet the internal elicitation of wonder also constitutes one of the powerful calls in fantasy, and its importance in producing the Coleridgean suspension of disbelief, of allowing the reader to become immersed in the story, should not be underestimated.

TWO TYPES OF WONDER

Put simply, there are two basic forms this Janus-like face of wonder takes. The first involves characters from our world, who are generally translated to another, magical world or less frequently encounter the seemingly impossible in ours;

they confront the marvelous and uncanny much as we would do and thereby stand in for us and serve as keys for our responses. A character such as the unremarkably named Bernard Brown of John Brunner's *Traveller in Black,* asked by the citizen of Ryorova to intercede for them, is "competent . . . in matters touching roads, drains and bridges and similar practical undertakings," hardly a heroic response. His initial reactions to the impossible experiences he encounters in the Traveller's world reflect Anyman's: disbelief, shock, and wide-eyed astonishment. Once he is established, despite his protests, among the local citizenry as a savior wizard or god, his observations, which are grounded in everyday experience in our primary world, create awe and veneration among the population, who return his wonder of them. Thus, their perception of their world (and their putative gods) undergoes a shift that brings them closer to our own, an example of the reflexive working of external and internal wonder.

Furthermore, those characters who remain in our recent or contemporary world reproduce or anticipate the reader's reactions. Real-world fantasies may well constitute the smallest body of fantasies, since high or heroic fantasy generally demands the alternate world. Brian Aldiss sardonically posits that "one principle of fantasy is to have the magic event happen far away. Not only does distance lend enchantment; it makes facts hard to check on." Yet fantasies set in the contemporary world do exist, and among acclaimed works set in a vaguely modern age (as opposed to the quasi-medieval prototype) are Mark Helprin's *Winter's Tale,* Matt Ruff's *Fool on the Hill,* Dan Simmons's World Fantasy award-winner *Song of Kali,* Michaela Roessner's *Walkabout Woman,* Peter Beagle's *A Fine and Private Place,* and Suzy McKee Charnas' *Dorothea Dreams.* Helprin's Peter Lake explores the incredible riches and potentialities of a lyrical and visionary New York City, for instance, which commingles the real with the ideal and leaves him overwhelmed. Roessner's aboriginal heroine Raba signals to us the exotic alienness and distance from our world of the Outback, which can captivate even without the supernatural, while her embassies into the Dreamtime of aboriginal myth add yet another dimension of wonder. Ruff's comic portrayal of university life, complete with a fraternity named Tolkien House and resident sprites in the library, is really about the wonder of discovery and of knowledge that one hopes for in all students, while Simmons' gruesome novel makes us cringe as it replays the ironic horror of the world we inhabit in which children are destroyed more horribly than in any invented world. An anodyne exists in Charnas' *Dorothea Dreams* when art, the sole magic medium left in our world, can save both children and adults from everyday dangers and problems we would all recognize. Her characters wonder, in the worst sense of the word, at each other until a greater wonder seizes and unites them all.

Where the application of real-world events to seeming impossible or incomprehensible behavior or events enjoys the greatest appeal and acceptance is in the subgenre of mass market horror that uses wonder as a stepping stone to terror. The shambling zombie, the vampire, the slithering monster, the invulnerable mutant, the BEM (bug-eyed monster) from hell—all would cause pacemakers to stop and cars to collide on Main Street, Anytown, after jaws dropped and eyes bulged. Perhaps one of Stephen King's greatest strengths lies in his workaday characters' fidelity to the average person's reactions and behavior before supernatural evil, as wonder, admixes with them and results in terror. Certainly *It*, flawed as the novel is by the midcourse shift from horror to science fiction, translates the seeds of every child's fears about adult strength, repression, and incomprehensibility, all of which the child must marvel at, into terms anyone can understand. H.P. Lovecraft appeals to similar responses in his shabby old towns beneath which timeless horrors lurk, waiting for someone, foolishly captivated by the promise of fascinating discovery, to release them; the perspective of the innocent and curious often dominates, and horror exudes from the gap between what is and what is imagined. On another level at times, comedy enters, for instance, in Nancy Collins's *Sunglasses after Dark* when Claude Hagerty is so amazed at what the vampire Sonia Blue can do that he actually forgets to be afraid of her—for a little while. As hoods sent by her enemies attempt to kill them, he sits—with broken bones—in amazement at her defense and then awakes to see a concerned vampire leaning over him (and his throat), trying to help.

A contrast to the principle I am discussing comes in Kafka's "Metamorphosis"; one of the continuing curiosities of this tale for me has always been Gregor Samsa's family's general acceptance of his transformation, for disgust, not wonder or terror, is the keynote here. Gregor wakes up as an "unge-heuer Ungeziefer," a giant bug or cockroach, yet his family does not call in the police, the secret service, or even a good entomologist. What gives here? Is Kafka's allegory of the ne-glected so close to us that it precludes wonder in favor of dis-gust at our daily world? Is Gregor, the functionary enmeshed in bestial servility along with his family, so common that wonder is, de facto, banished? Why is the marvel of Gregor's transformation subjugated to other concerns? I suspect that Kafka's intent is to show us that we are so complacent or so reluctant to deal with the new or unusual so that making Gregor's metamorphosis "fantastic" would undermine his social critique. The only one who seems to wonder about what has happened to Gregor is Gregor; in fact, his morbidly funny discovery of a roach's mobility (and his pleasure therein) twitches the novelette in line with other fantasies.

For in all the previous works, it seems clear that internal wonder's direct functions are to induce reader identification and comprehension through vicarious experiences and to bring the fantasy world into contrast with the everyday one, so perhaps little more need be said about it. Yet in the second type of internal wonder, that exhibited by the inhabitants of the astounding world, the same does not hold true, and other forces are at work. The reactions of characters native to sec-ondary worlds again ally them to us but in different ways; in this group members, even magical ones, of the various races of fantasy—elves, dwarves, giants, mer-creatures, goblins, trolls, men of various sorts, and so on—are captivated by the marvels of their own world. Because they are not inhabitants of our world, their response to the secondary world height-ens and deepens our own. Moreover, their feelings and reac-tions provide a bedrock on which the first class of wonder can be built. If the inhabitants of Faerie stand in wide-eyed astonishment at the rivers, mountains, creatures, battles, or magical events of their world, certainly they draw both mor-tal visitors and readers into understanding the primary and secondary worlds in terms of each other.

CREATING A WONDROUS SETTING

For the worlds are paramount. Perhaps fantasy's most pow-erful attraction for readers resides in the wonder of the fan-tasyscape, especially since many of the plots are redundant and formulaic and the characters imitations of established types and archetypes. Thus, appreciation of the marvelous world must be crafted through both external and internal expressions of wonder, if it is to be effective and efficient. We expect denizens of our world to be openmouthed at the beauty and bounty, or the terror and evil, of the fantasy worlds to which they are transported. As Raymond Thompson puts it, "The splendor of the new surroundings consequently gains from the wonder it inspires in these travellers from less exotic regions." If the children of C.S. Lewis's Narnia books saunter into that country as though into the town green, wonder flees before the grotty ogre of didacticism. If Stephen Donaldson's Thomas Covenant and later Linden Avery are not moved by the grandeur of the Land, they become spectral figures whose experiences we might well resent, since they would seem clearly unworthy of them. Much of the effect of Olaf Stapledon's *Star Maker* resides in both the emotional and philosophical outpourings of the unnamed narrator who is inspired by the alternate worlds he visits. Such figures' sense of awe, surprise, and admiration co-creates our own in the truest Wordsworthian sense by evoking things not before our eyes but held in our minds and hearts.

Characters not of our world who live in the sub-created fantasy world marvel at the spectacles and mysteries in their own existence and experiences. Certainly, the appearance of the oliphaunt does not have the same effect on us that it has on Sam the hobbit. The beast is merely a larger version of what we all have seen, whereas Sam himself is an occasion of wonder, being a smaller version of what we have never seen. Even the maps Tolkien lovingly and intricately details function differently in and out of the narrative. To hobbits, wizards, dwarves, and elves alike they are treasured heirlooms with powers and conundrums of their own, often magic-laden relics to be pored over with careful devotion. Frodo and Bilbo especially are fascinated and drawn by them. To us, as readers, they are primarily guides, certainly captivating ones, but lacking the emotional impact they have on the characters in Middle Earth, since we cannot, as they say in Maine, get there from here. And I have little doubt that every serious reader of fantasy has at one time or another finished a book and wanted to write the author an irritated or plaintive note asking for a map or even for better maps, simply from a more pedestrian type of wondering.

As I pointed out before, those who do not live in Narnia,

Prydain, Middle Earth, the Land, Fionavar, the Enchanted Forest, or any of their magical parallels should react with wonder because of the strangeness of the new environment. But what of the typical fantasy character to whom magic is a familiar accompaniment to everyday life? What of those adepts and powerful mages who control such forces? What function does their awe play in the creation of our own or in the creation of the secondary world? For they too react with wonder and incredulous appreciation before the marvels of their worlds: Aragorn wandering as if dazed through Lorien, Gimli elevated to rhetorical exuberance at the caves in Helm's Deep; Faramir moved beyond grief, worry, and fear at Frodo's announcement of his errand. Standing before the majesty of Revelstone, Saltheart Foamfollower's delight and amazement surpass Covenant's although as a Giant he is kin to those who built it, and even those who dwell in it—the Lords, soldiers, and citizens—never cease to marvel at its power. In Kay's Fionavar trilogy, as the unicorn walks through Pendaran Wood "among the gathered powers, seen and unseen, a murmur like the forest's answer to the sea had risen up and fallen like a wave in the wood." In Roger Zelazny's Amber, one distinguishing characteristic is the awe that even the hardheaded and devious princes and princesses feel when they have returned to Amber itself as opposed to their pedestrian view of our Earth. In Ursula Le Guin's Earthsea, all marvel at, even as they worry about, dragons. Toward the end of his journey with Ged, Arren sees dragons far beyond the reaches of man, "and his heart leapt up then with them with a joy, a joy of fulfillment, that was like pain"; and he thinks to himself, "I do not care what comes after; I have seen dragons on the wind of morning." Even John Brunner's demigod, the Traveler in Black, at times himself stands in admiration or wonder as he makes his appointed rounds.

This type of internal wonder operates beyond the yoking of the reader's experience to that of the characters', although it plays a supporting role there too. Since one of the foremost concerns of the fantasy author is the construction of the secondary world, if it does not ring true, the fiction will not succeed. Rabkin insists that the internal ground rules of fantasy must be consistent. One stipulation must, therefore, be the establishment of formal realism for internal response. A fantasy world cannot be concomitantly mundane and fascinating, and its inhabitants must be moved by its properties. Their response, as an internal patterning, helps us to understand fantasy in terms of what Sir Herbert Read calls "extraverted feeling." Here, paradoxically enough, the effects arise from an internally generated feeling that is transformed into an external response for the reader.

Thus, what exists in our world must be reproduced in the other, yet separated and distinguished from it at the same time. Attebery points out that "to recover our sense of something like a tree, it is only necessary to envision a dragon curled around its trunk." If we place amazed dwellers of that world around both the tree and the dragon, both take on greater depth, as do the observers themselves, yet it is not simply the juxtaposition of dragon-tree observers that allows recovery or revitalization of the idea of tree; the astonishment or sense of the sublime that comes from those observers endows the entire scene with life beyond the verbal portrait of dragon and tree.

THE CHARACTERS THEMSELVES INCITE WONDER

In such ways the various wonderful beings of Faerie contribute to the efficacy of a secondary creation. Gary Wolfe tells us that "in an effective fantasy work we do not lose our sense of the wondrous or impossible even long after all the marvels have been introduced and the magic has become commonplace." Much of this effect must be produced by the construction of internal wonder. Elves are of themselves a source of amazement to many characters in fantasy, yet they also testify to wonder and help create different levels of perception. We cannot, hobbits cannot, dwarves cannot see as elves see in their world; their vision thereby expands ours. An elf lost in wonder, mazed by beauty or sorrow, can only intensify the impact of the scene or event. Similarly, a wizard or mage enchanted by some lost periapt or exposition of magical power brings the object or act into a different focus than if it called for only casual scrutiny. Michael Scott Rohan's mastersmith Elof stands astounded at his own creations and skill; their reality is a source of pride and yet amazement in him. And warriors grow in stature as a result of the reactions of those around them; even Beowulf's own men shake their heads in disbelief at both Grendel's arm and their leader's handy removal thereof.

For their world is one of discovery as well so that as each

character uncovers the new and marvelous, his or her reaction is passed on to the reader. One popular and pervasive fantasy paradigm centers on a naive and inexperienced hero who takes a voyage to grow into his or her potential, so by necessity he or she must meet incredible beings and places previously undreamt of: dragons, trolls, talking trees, walking stones, magical doors, shape-changing creatures, and so on. Bilbo and Frodo, Ged, Morgon of Patricia McKillip's "Riddlemaster" novels, Jane Yolen's White Jenna, and countless others fit this pattern. Part of their education consists of being introduced to the wonders of their world by a parental figure, an archetype of wisdom, a Gandalf or an Ogion, who teaches them the value of knowledge and the never-ending wonders of the world around them.

Wonder, however, is a two-edged sword that poses difficulties for an author. Some fantasies seem to strive for an endless series of prodigies at which the characters ooh and ahh in bathetic reverence. In an early article on the nature of fantasy, Jane Mobley identifies "essential extravagance" as one of fantasy's predominant characteristics: "The language of fantasy is itself extravagant, creating oftentimes by the mere unpronounceability of names the wonder and greatness of it all." Yet I think this is an overstatement, for this essential extravagance all too frequently is the mark of bad fantasy, of shoddy imitations. Brian Aldiss warns of this sort of writing. Concocting a fictional writer named Astrid Stanza, he posits a situation in which she writes at the behest of an editor who "suggests that quest stories are popular at present; perhaps a quest in which Innocent [sic] has to overcome Evil and the young Witch Maiden saves the universe." To make the story more exciting, she has her "characters cry such things as 'Welladay'" and gives them "difficult and unmemorable names of not more than two syllables: Scrant, Gremte, Gringi, 'vizzil, and so on." As arcane or affected language stands in for world-building and craftsmanship, each weir or bosk ravishes the assaulted sense beyond the power of the last; each selkie, ghole, or tantarrabob outdoes its predecessor in minatory ghastliness; each sylvan Phaery sprite whorls in dance, trailing nacreous gloamings of moondew. In such cases, overreaching brings down all, for the attempt to make everything wonder-filled cannot be sustained. To emphasize everything, of course, is ultimately to emphasize nothing.

On the other hand, a different weakness in many fantasies, especially in the myriad Tolkien imitations, in the merely formulaic and redundant sagas of noble elves, grumpy dwarves, and good people, is lack of wonder, most notably internal wonder simply because all has been reduced to preestablished or preapproved conventions. Most of the characters in such works go blithely about their business, and the things that produce wonder in other stories here simply form windowdressings. There is no sense of estrangement, or even of "essential extravagance" with a function, no miracle or marvelous edging into the unknown or reknown. Such books and tales reduce themselves to a Dungeons and Dragons proposition of playing at elves and dwarves, as if of ducks and drakes. Certainly, their author-creators can fill them with wondrous beings, objects, and events, all directed toward the reader's sensibility; but without an effective internal wonder filigreed into the structure of things, these outward shows all fail. The Pickwickian Sam confronted with the glorious oliphaunt becomes a Gradgrindian, utilitarian Sam who sees only a quadruped, graminiverous, pachydermous, possessed of tusks and trunk, habitat generally subtropical. Such an unfortunate creature has been dispossessed not only of wonder but of reality itself. Fantasy, through the medium of wonder, not only allows us to see things as they aren't; it lets us realize things as they are—from the inside out.

Symbolism and Allegory

Ann Swinfen

Ann Swinfen, lecturer and tutor for the Open University in England and author of *In Defence of Fantasy*, has found that symbolism and allegory play a large role in many fantasy novels. In Swinfen's view most fantasy authors rely on the established symbolism of fairy tales, but the best writers are those that shape the symbol to their particular story without losing the associations that symbol has in the reader's value system. Sometimes, as Swinfen notes, authors incorporate symbolism into their stories to impart a value system. In this case the stories become allegories, attempting to teach readers moral lessons.

Fantasy, being of its nature a form of multivalent writing, naturally makes considerable use of allegory and symbolism. Allegory is not popular, or at any rate it has not been so during the period of dominance of the realist novel. Moreover, modern writing in the allegorical mode, such as that of Kafka, Orwell, Huxley, or Mervyn Peake, tends to reflect the collapse of universal belief and the confusion and fragmentation of moral standards in modern Western society. Such allegories tend to be critical and destructive, rather than emulative and creative. Man is no longer seen as faced with a divinely ordered universe in which he may achieve salvation or damnation through his virtuous adaptation to or sinful rebellion against the God-given plan. Rather he is seen as an individualist who must discover his own morality and defy the man-made structures and hierarchies which are devised to destroy his individual integrity. This kind of modern allegorical writing occurs in modern fantasy; so also does traditional Christian allegory, and both will be considered later in this chapter.

In fantasy the symbolic element is in general closely related to the elements of the marvellous, and is used to provide that wider frame of reference which has already been illustrated as characteristic of the genre. Jonathan Raban discusses this quality with regard to the realist novel, but his remarks gain even more force in relation to the fantasy novel:

> a fabric of symbolism may enable the writer to create a moral and intellectual framework for the action of his novel. Symbolism allows an author to link the limited world of his characters to one of the great systems of values, so that we are made to compare the happenings in the novel with their mythological or historical parallels. Specific actions in the story illustrate general patterns of behaviour, and the private character acquires a new importance when he is seen in the light of his symbolic counterpart.

Many writers of fantasy draw on traditional symbolism, from mythology, folk-tale and Christian religion, or on the nature symbolism of the Romantics. One principal reason for using such established forms of imagery was discussed by Alan Garner:

> I begin to suspect that I use fantasy and mythology because I am not good enough to do without it. I need some kind of crutch, some kind of framework, I suspect. My most reputable reason for doing it is that myth is not an attempt to entertain, it is an attempt to explain something. Originally people did not sit around and cook up fairy stories to get through the long winter evenings. They were trying to come to terms with their environment, so you find that over the millenia [sic] myth contains crystallized human experience and very powerful imagery. This imagery is useful for a writer if he uses it responsibly. It can work against him if he does not use it properly, but if he uses it correctly then he has very powerful cutting tools in his hand which work beneath the surface.

SYMBOLISM IN THE WORK OF LLOYD ALEXANDER

A number of these 'very powerful cutting tools' are used by Lloyd Alexander in *The Chronicles of Prydain*. Alexander himself is aware of the danger of 'improvization' and an over-abundance of fantasy—'Enchanted swords, wielded incautiously, cut both ways.' The marvellous elements of Prydain are closely linked with the symbolism. Cauldrons with magical properties are common in folklore, one of the best known being that in *The Juniper Tree,* in which the little boy is boiled up into soup for his unsuspecting father by a cruel stepmother. His loving stepsister, however, buries the bones under the juniper tree, and the boy is resurrected first as a bird, and eventually as himself. The cauldron in *The Mabinogion*, from which Alexander drew his inspiration, is also associated with rebirth after death. The Irish throw into it the dead bodies of their warriors, 'and on the morrow they would arise as good fighting men as before, save that they were not able to speak.'

In *The Book of Three*, the first of Alexander's *Chronicles of Prydain*, Arawn the Death-Lord has stolen the cauldron of rebirth from the three fatal sisters of the marshes of Morva, and used it to create fighters for his own evil cause by casting into it the bodies of noble enemies, who emerge as the silent and deathless Cauldron-Born. In the second book, *The Black Cauldron*, Arawn is no longer content to rob graves: 'his servants dare to strike down the living and bear them to Annuvin to swell the ranks of his deathless host. Thus, death begets death; evil begets evil.'

It is the young hero Taran who finds the cauldron, once more in the possession of the fatal sisters. . . . To gain the cauldron, Taran exchanges for it his most precious possession, the brooch of Adaon. And he learns that to destroy the cauldron will cost not a brooch, but a life:

> 'A living person must climb into it,' Orddu said. 'When he does, the Crochan will shatter. . . . Not only that, but whoever gives up his life to the Crochan must give it willingly, knowing full well what he does.'

In *The Mabinogion* the repentant traitor Efnisien feigns death in order to burst the cauldron from within. *The Black Cauldron* also contains an anti-hero, the bitter, twisted and occasionally traitorous Ellidyr. Ellidyr steals the Crochan from Taran in order to win the glory for himself, but both he and the cauldron fall into the hands of Morgant, would-be rival of Arawn. Repenting of his treachery at last, Ellidyr manages to leap willingly into the cauldron and his sacrifice destroys the Crochan, which robbed the dead of peace and turned good men to evil. Alexander has thus widened the reference of the symbolic cauldron on the moral level. Efnisien was thrown into the cauldron of *The Mabinogion* at his own desire, and destroyed it by physical strength. It is the strength of the willing sacrifice itself which shatters the Crochan of Prydain. . . .

SYMBOLISM IN LEWIS'S NARNIA SERIES

C.S. Lewis also makes some use of mythological symbolism in *The Chronicles of Narnia*, but the Christian symbolism is much more prominent and central. The most potent and pervasive of these symbols is Aslan, the lion symbol of Christ. Dorothy Sayers, attacking a reviewer who complained that Aslan should have been given 'the shape as well as the nature and functions of an archangel,' pointed out the incorrect assumptions which lay behind this remark as well as the suitability of Aslan as a symbol for Christ:

> The Lion Aslan . . . has most emphatically *not* the 'nature and functions' of an archangel, and for that reason has not been given the form of one. In these tales of Absolutely Elsewhere, Aslan is shown as creating the worlds *(The Magician's Nephew)*, slain and risen again for the redemption of sin *(The Lion, the Witch and the Wardrobe)*, incarnate as a Talking Beast among Talking Beasts *(passim)*, and obedient to the laws he has made for his own creation *(The Voyage of the 'Dawn Treader')*. His august Archetype—higher than the angels and 'made a little lower' than they—is thus readily identified as the 'Lion of the Tribe of Judah'. Apart from a certain disturbance of the natural hierarchies occasioned by the presence of actual human beings, Professor Lewis's theology and pneumatology are as accurate and logical here as in his other writings.

Aslan is both 'good and terrible at the same time.' Full of energy and creative power, he also has elements in his nature of the Old Testament Jehovah, god of vengeance.

In the figures of Jadis, priestess queen and White Witch, and of the Green Lady, Queen of the Underland and occasionally poisonous serpent, Lewis combines the folklore and medieval romance type of the beautiful but evil enchantress with elements from Christian mythology. Jadis attempts to gain her ends through threats of violence, and when that fails resorts to temptation—unsuccessfully with Digory under the Tree of Life in the paradisal Garden, successfully with Edmund, who is already partially corrupted. The Green Lady sometimes manifests herself openly as a poisonous serpent whose bite is deadly, but more often she works more subtly, undermining belief by dreamy enchantment and sweetly reasonable linguistic analysis. Underworld comes to symbolize this earth, full of unhappy, cowed, half-blind Earthmen, who either deny or fear the existence of Overworld—the transcendent heavenly reality. The Green

Lady tries to destroy the belief of the children, Puddleglum and the disenchanted Rilian, in the very existence of Overworld, its sun, and Aslan, by arguing that they are only a game of make-believe.

Sometimes the Christian symbolism is used quite briefly, as when the stable takes on a new significance in *The Last Battle*, when believers and unbelievers are hurled through it:

> 'It seems, then,' said Tirian . . . 'that the Stable seen from within and the Stable seen from without are two different places.'
>
> 'Yes,' said the Lord Digory. 'Its inside is bigger than its outside.'
>
> 'Yes,' said Queen Lucy. 'In our world too, a Stable once had something inside it that was bigger than our whole.'

THE MOVE TOWARD ALLEGORY

On the other hand, in a number of places *The Chronicles of Narnia* move into full allegory. . . . His Christian symbolism is clear cut, his Christian allegories form set-pieces which can easily be isolated and discussed. The Creation, the Passion, the Apocalypse and Day of Judgment are presented by Lewis as straightforward allegories, although, with curious disingenuousness, he denied that the Narnia books *were* allegories.

Although *The Lion, the Witch and the Wardrobe* may have had its very first genesis, as Lewis maintained, in a series of 'pictures' in the mind, yet by the time he came to write it, many years later, he had much more clearly developed intentions. He had already written a number of works of Christian apologetics and his planetary romances with their strongly didactic element. Before embarking on his first Narnian novel, he was very much influenced by reading a manuscript novel by Roger Lancelyn Green. Here, clearly, was an intriguing form, the fantasy novel, in which Lewis could express his views on Christianity. Unfortunately, the element of didacticism is so strong, the events allegorized of such cosmic importance, and Lewis's interest in them so much stronger than his interest in such aspects of his novels as the child heroes and heroines, that the allegorical elements are out of all proportion with the rest of the *Chronicles*. Moreover, the didacticism is too thinly disguised, and sometimes positively distasteful. The result is that the Narnia books are an uneasy and uneven mixture, and the passages of allegory float like stubborn lumps in a rather thin gruel. . . .

JUSTER AND OVERT ALLEGORY

Norton Juster's *The Phantom Tollbooth* is . . . an allegory of the development of the mind. Milo is a typical modern little boy: surrounded with a plentiful supply of toys and mechanical gadgets, he has never learned to use either his mental capacities or his physical senses. He rushes from home to school and back again, locked in his boredom and blind to the world about him. When he finds in his room a mysterious package labelled 'For Milo, who has plenty of time,' containing a tollbooth, he decides he might as well play with it, for lack of anything better to do. Driving past the tollbooth in his pedal car, Milo suddenly finds himself in the Kingdom of Wisdom.

The Phantom Tollbooth is unusual both in being an overt allegory and in being openly and avowedly didactic. Yet the whole form and style of the book are so witty that there is no sense of oppressive didacticism. The reader, like Milo, is made aware of the beauty and the fun of both words and numbers, as the verbal pyrotechnics carry him forward through the Kingdom of Wisdom. In the prison of the city of Dictionopolis, Faintly Macabre, the not-so-wicked Which and great-aunt of King Azaz the Unabridged, explains the right use of words to Milo and his companion, the Watchdog Tock. Faintly Macabre was formerly the Official Which, in charge of choosing the correct words to use on all occasions, until power made her miserly, and she banned the use of all words. Repentant now, she tells Milo: 'they never appointed a new Which, and that explains why today people use as many words as they can and think themselves very wise for doing so. For always remember that while it is wrong to use too few, it is often far worse to use too many.'

Setting out later from the city of Digitopolis, ruled by the Mathemagician, Milo, Tock and the Humbug struggle up the mountains of Ignorance in order to bring back the exiled Princesses Rhyme and Reason, and rescue the Kingdom of Wisdom from chaos. Their way is barred by the Terrible Trivium, 'demon of petty tasks and worthless jobs, ogre of wasted effort and monster of habit.' Milo recalls how much of his life has been spent doing unimportant things, and the Trivium urges them to stay with him: 'If you only do the easy and useless jobs, you'll never have to worry about the important ones which are so difficult. You just won't have the time. For there's always something to do to keep you from what you really should be doing, and if it weren't for that dreadful magic staff, you'd never know how much time you were wasting.' Here too they encounter the Senses Taker, who demands that they fill in endless forms, telling him: 'When you were born, where you were born, why you were born, how old you are now, how old you were then, how old you'll be in a little while, your mother's name, your father's name, your aunt's name, your uncle's name, your cousin's name, where you live, how long you've lived there, the schools you've attended, the schools you haven't attended. . . .'

As his questions indicate, the Senses Taker epitomizes that aspect of modern life which destroys privacy and diminishes the worth of the individual. He is concerned to misdirect people's energies, so that they become hopelessly entangled in a web of trivia:

> 'I help people find what they're *not* looking for, hear what they're *not* listening for, run after what they're *not* chasing, and smell what isn't even there. And furthermore, . . . I'll steal your sense of purpose, take your sense of duty, destroy your sense of proportion—and, but for one thing, you'd be helpless yet.'

> 'What's that?' asked Milo fearfully.

> 'As long as you have the sound of laughter,' he groaned unhappily, 'I cannot take your sense of humour—and, with it, you've nothing to fear from me.'

Not only is the stress on mental agility and the ability to distinguish between words used to communicate ideas and words used to confuse. Milo is also brought to a keen sense of the world about him, mainly through sight and sound, but also through taste, touch and smell. Alec Bings, who can see 'whatever is inside, behind, around, covered by or subsequent to anything else,' explains to Milo that 'it's just as bad to live in a place where what you do see isn't there as it is to live in one where what you don't see is.' The capacity to perceive the physical world aright is thus linked with the power to distinguish between reality and illusion. 'Perhaps some day you can have one city as easy to see as Illusions and as hard to forget as Reality,' Milo answers.

The subtle relationships between colours and moods are evoked in the scene with Chroma's orchestra, which is responsible for washing in all the colour in what would otherwise be a grey and featureless landscape. Having watched Chroma conduct the sunset, Milo decides to try to conduct the dawn:

> The 'cellos made the hills glow red, and the leaves and grass
> were tipped with a soft pale green as the violins began their
> song. Only the bass fiddles rested as the entire orchestra
> washed the forest in colour.

In the Valley of Sound, Milo discovers the results of the mis-
use of sound, in a sharply pointed allegory of modern life,
where the senses are so often dulled to the world around.
The Soundkeeper, who used to rule wisely and well, has
grown disgusted at the behaviour of the people in the valley:

> She was generous to a fault and provided us with all the
> sound we could possibly use: for singing as we worked, for
> bubbling pots of stew, for the chop of an axe and the crash of
> a tree, for the creak of a hinge and the hoot of an owl, for the
> squish of a shoe in the mud and the friendly tapping of rain
> on the roof, and for the sweet music of pipes and the sharp
> snap of winter ice cracking on the ground. . . . Slowly at first,
> and then in a rush, more people came to settle here and
> brought with them new ways and new sounds, some very
> beautiful and some less so. But everyone was so busy with
> the things that had to be done that they scarcely had time to
> listen at all. And, as you know, a sound which is not heard
> disappears for ever and is not to be found again.
>
> People laughed less and grumbled more, sang less and
> shouted more, and the sounds they made grew louder and
> uglier. It became difficult to hear even the birds or the breeze,
> and soon everyone stopped listening for them.

To punish the inhabitants of the valley, the Soundkeeper has
locked up all the sounds in the filing cabinets in her fortress
and refuses to release them until reconciled with the people
of the valley by Milo's efforts.

What is eminently satisfying about *The Phantom Tollbooth* is that it requires of the reader exactly that mental
alertness, both to the surface complexities and to the deeper
levels of meaning, which is the theme of the allegory. With
its insistence on the right use of words—neither hoarding
them nor over-spending—and the right use of the reasoning
and mathematical faculty of the mind, it becomes an almost
archetypal allegory, an allegory of the way in which Rhyme
and Reason together maintain the right balance in the realm
of Wisdom. . . .

MAKING REALITY TRANSCENDENT

One quality is shared by all the books discussed here—a
quality to be found in most fantasies, but especially strong in
those which employ sustained symbolism or allegory. It is

the desire to communicate to the reader a vision of some kind of transcendent reality. The primary world is seen as possessing an intense beauty of its own, which is too often neglected within the circumscribed boundaries of modern life. At the same time, the beauties of the primary world are in some sense, and in different ways and degrees for different writers, only a shadow, a temporal manifestation of a luminous and eternal reality. Milo is made aware of the first side of this vision:

> He noticed somehow that the sky was a lovely shade of blue and that one cloud had the shape of a sailing ship. The tips of the trees held pale, young buds and the leaves were a rich deep green. Outside the window, there was so much to see, and hear, and touch—walks to take, hills to climb, caterpillars to watch as they strolled through the garden. There were voices to hear and conversations to listen to in wonder, and the special smell of each day.
>
> And, in the very room in which he sat, there were books that could take you anywhere, and things to invent, and make, and build, and break, and all the puzzle and excitement of everything he didn't know—music to play, songs to sing, and worlds to imagine and then some day make real. His thoughts darted eagerly about as everything looked new— and worth trying. . . .

[These books reveal] the essential elements of the multilevel fantasy: the vision of the individual's life within the primary world, seen with sharpness of detail, but set within a framework of continuity and wholeness, and the vision of a secondary world of metaphysical reality, unattainable in this life, but constantly enhancing the individual's perception and experience of primary world reality.

The Quest

John H. Timmerman

John H. Timmerman, fantasy scholar, author, and
English professor, recognizes that the quest for adventure is the foundation for much of ancient literature and mythology. But in the fantasy genre the
quest is not merely for adventure, it is a serious undertaking when life or society is gravely threatened.
While Timmerman digs deep into various types of
fantasy to define the quest, he also examines the
significance of the journey itself and the importance
of longing.

Ancient literatures and mythologies frequently based the action of a story upon a quest. In place of the quest, modern literature has often provided an adventure. The distinction lies
at the heart of fantasy. If the fantasy hero must act . . . he
must often seek long and desperately for a basis for action.
The question which this hero pursues is different from an
adventure in several significant ways. In the first place, an
adventure may lead anywhere. Jack Kerouac's *On The Road*
is an adventure; the road takes the rider out, but the rider
has no precise goal. The quest is always *toward* something,
although that something often becomes clear only with the
seeking of it. Second, the adventure may be undertaken for
any number of reasons—boredom with one's present situation, a wanderlust, a dissatisfaction with things as they are.
The quest, however, is always a spiritual or religious undertaking. The quest hero is appointed or ordained to his mis-
sion, and its end has spiritual significance. Third, the adventure may be merely a whimsical frolic. In contrast, the
quest is always a grave, serious undertaking. It is often life-
threatening, marked by a sense of struggle, of imminent or
immediate danger in which the character must call upon all
of his will and power to push on.

The goal of fantasy is to lead the reader to a keener un-

Excerpted from *Other Worlds: The Fantasy Genre*, by John H. Timmerman. Copyright
© 1983 by Bowling Green University Popular Press. Reprinted with permission from
Bowling Green University Popular Press.

derstanding of himself and his world. Adventure often follows a path along which the reader may lose himself and his world. When Dylan Thomas wrote

Twenty-four years remind the tears of my eyes.
In the final direction of the elementary town
I advance for as long as forever is

I suspect that through the verbal larding that fattens his work, Thomas was in search for that sacred altar of self-understanding. Recent biographies confirm my suspicion. Often in his turbulent, pub-crawling lifetime, Thomas retreated to the cottage at Blaen Cwm. The poems written there groped toward a way he would not go. When he described a saviour as "rarer than radium/commoner than water, crueller than truth," the saviour was nothing more than words full of pretty sounds. The Blaen Cwm, his writing haven, was *only* a hideaway. It was never a place from which he began anew. Fantasy provides not a hiding place but a point from which the reader can begin anew. The fantasy artist expects the reader to learn something about himself by having made a sojourn through fantasy. The writer invites the reader to probe his spiritual nature, to grow in experience, to resolve himself to new directions. The quest provides a basis for such exploration.

Defining a True Quest

In a convincing essay W.H. Auden establishes the nature of the "true quest" in literary tradition. "To look for a lost button," argues Auden, "is not a true quest." Why not? In the first place, because one knows precisely what he is looking for. Furthermore, the button is something once held in possession, and it can be regained in several ways. If one fails to find the button, a near duplicate may be purchased, or the coat from which it has been lost may be serviceable without the button, or the coat may be simply discarded. "To go in quest," Auden writes, "means to look for something of which one has, as yet, no experience; one can imagine what it will be like but whether one's picture is true or false will be known only when one has found it."

The quest is one of the oldest literary forms. Greek heroic mythology is predicated upon its action. In fact, David Leeming notes in *Mythology: The Voyage of the Hero* that: "The quest myth in one sense is the *only* myth—that is, all other myths are a part of the quest myth. The hero's whole life from birth to apotheosis is a quest, whether for an actual place or object in this world, as is the case with Odysseus and Jason, or for eternal life in another world, as is the case with the great religious leaders such as Jesus and Quetzal-coatl." Northrop Frye has similarly argued that "all literary genres are derived from the quest myth." Surely the quest has had a profound impact upon modern literature. Byron used Manfred, Prometheus, and Childe Harold to exemplify his own tortured seeking. Browning gave us Roland winding his horn before a desolate tower. Camus' Sisyphus guides all of his work. Auden's achievement is to establish the following essential traits which unify the many variations of the quest from its earliest forms to its latest descendents:

1) A precious Object and/or Person to be found and possessed or married.

2) A long journey to find it, for its whereabouts are not originally known.

3) A hero. The precious Object cannot be found by anybody, but only by the one person who possesses the right qualities of breeding or character.

4) A Test or series of Tests by which the unworthy are screened out, and the hero revealed.

5) The Guardians of the Object who must be overcome before it can be won. They may be simply a further test of the hero's *arete*, or they may be malignant in themselves.

6) The Helpers who with their knowledge and magical powers assist the hero and but for whom he would never succeed. They may appear in human or in animal form.

Auden's traits are an essential minimum for defining the quest. Although one particular trait may be given greater emphasis in any particular story, all must be present to some degree. However, Auden omits one essential trait which forms the background for any quest—a threat to the status quo. Quests are pursued only when grave events threaten the well-being of a society. This is true in ancient literature as well as modern fantasy. No quest is pursued for the sheer fun of it. The qualification is important since an adventure is often undertaken simply because the status quo has become torpid in its uneventfulness and the adventurer is motivated by little more than accentuated ennui. In the quest, the threat to the status quo often makes the hero long for the routine, and frequently the quest is pursued in order to recover that state.

It is true that what begins in adventure may end in a quest. Tolkien's *The Hobbit* appears at first to be adventure. Bilbo Baggins is disturbed from his routine by an unexpected visit and, as unexpectedly, finds himself on a voyage. Not until the graver implications of the arkenstone emerge, does the adventure become more universal in significance. Then Bilbo longs for the commonplace life of the shire, but he also realizes that such life cannot be regained without completing the quest. *The Hobbit* is rather unusual in its use of the quest, quite different for example, from *The Lord of the Rings* which begins in a situation of ominous events in which the threat is immediately present. . . .

THE JOURNEY IS WHAT MATTERS

It has become fashionable in mainstream contemporary literature to have a character pursue a quest without finding any sure or certain answers, and thereby to posit that there is no clearly discernible answer available to man in this world. One may argue that this is not a quest at all in the true sense. Yet the Romantic legacy of unrequited longing has left its imprint on the modern mind. And the Victorian revolutionaries engraved it irrevocably. Robert Browning left us not only the portrait of Roland winding his horn before the deserted tower, but also these famous lines from "Andrea Del Sarto": "Ah, but a man's reach should exceed his grasp,/Or what's a heaven for?"

The revolutionary fervor of Victorian thinkers was accepted by twentieth-century existentialists as a cause in itself. Change, they cried, for the sake of change. Seek, for the sake of seeking.

This sense of ceaseless questing has pervaded modern existential literature. In his *Myth of Sisyphus,* Camus depicts the old hero ceaselessly striving to push his boulder heavenward. Camus comments: "The struggle itself toward the heights is enough to fill a man's heart. One must imagine Sisyphus happy." Happiness lies in the seeking itself; not necessarily in the location of a goal. In effect, existential literature has ripped the heart out of Auden's scheme: the precious object to be discovered no longer exists.

One might argue that the precious object is man himself. That is a sound argument, and a pertinent one when one also accepts Lev Shestov's argument that "Necessity," the trait of our modern age in his view, denies man his own being. In fantasy the precious object is finally a "regained clarity," to use Tolkien's term, of man himself in his present world. But fantasy insists that the quest does have a goal, that it does have direction, that the seeker is actively directed by divine, supernatural aids in locating that goal. The fantasy hero is not forsaken to a barren world of pointless seeking. In temperament modern existentialism is rooted in the Romantic revolution against established and unvarying order. Fantasy . . . shares some of that same Romantic soil for its literary groundwork, but it is a different flower in the garden. An interesting literary link, and one which is illuminating of the fantasy quest, may be found between the Romantic poet Novalis, the early fantasist George MacDonald, and C.S. Lewis.

THE LONGING

Novalis, a self-confessed votary of the cult associated with the "Quest for the Blue Flower," a term that symbolizes an insatiable longing for an ideal which always seems just out of reach, was a powerful influence on George MacDonald. In fact, MacDonald wrote: "Shall I not one day, 'somewhere, somehow,' clasp the large hand of Novalis, and, gazing on his face, compare his features with those of Saint John?" And in a preface to one of MacDonald's works, Lewis wrote that "Novalis is perhaps the greatest single influence on MacDonald—full of 'holiness,' gloriously German-romantic." It is not unusual, perhaps, that the open-ended seeking of Novalis should influence the mystic sensibility of MacDonald. It is curious, however, that Lewis claimed MacDonald as his spiritual and literary mentor in much the same way that MacDonald did Novalis. Lewis wrote, for example, that what MacDonald's *Phantastes* "actually did to me was to convert, even to baptize . . . my imagination."

MacDonald wrote *Phantastes* during two months of a particularly frenetic and critical year (1858) of his life. This work, more than any other, haunted Lewis's youth. *The Pilgrim's Regress* shows the direct result of this influence, specifically in development of this theme of unrequited longing, which Lewis calls *Sehnsucht* in deference to Novalis. In "The Fantastic Imagination in George MacDonald" Glenn Sadler points out several affinities between the two works:

> MacDonald's *Phantastes* is a poet's artistic diary of youthful dreams. Like Lewis's *Pilgrim Regress*, it is the record of a

young man's spiritual contest with the "false objects" which taunt his thirst for the fulfillment of "Sweet Desire." Both Anodos and John search bravely for a realization in their actual life of dream-world aspirations. Both must forsake parental ties. Having strayed "far away from home John hears the plucking sound of the Aeolian harp beckoning him to "'Come.'" Through a glassless window he sees, for the first time, the primrose woods of Desire. . . .

Reflecting at a later date on his first reading of *Phantastes,* Lewis recognized the dangers inherent in this romantic longing: "I had already been waist-deep in Romanticism; and likely enough, at any moment, to flounder into its darker and more evil forms, slithering down the steep descent that leads from the love of strangeness to that of eccentricity and thence to that of perversity." Lewis, then, recognizes this longing and questing in his own personality and work, but also recognizes the danger of simply acting on this longing without any sense of direction. The distinction may be stated thus: romantic and existential seeking are often induced by a profound sense of alienation in this world and the effort somehow to appease one's own loneliness and longing. Thus, such seeking is inner-directed. The quest may originate from the same sense of alienation in this world, but its effort is somehow to rectify the situation in the world itself. The quest then is never individual, but social. One man may engage it; but he engages it for others.

In *Out of the Silent Planet* Lewis distinguishes between quests and individual longing by use of the terms *wondelone* and *hluntheline:* "These were two verbs which both, as far as he could see, meant to *long* or *yearn;* but the *hrossa* [creatures of the planet Mars] drew a sharp distinction, even an opposition, between them. Hyoi seemed to him merely to be saying that every one would long for it *(wondelone)* but no one in his senses could long for it *(hluntheline).*" In this case *wondelone* is akin to the seeking of the quest, while *hluntheline* is conceived as the seeking of self-gratification. The distinction is further defined in this passage from *Perelandra:*

> As he let the empty gourd fall from his hand and was about to pluck a second one, it came into his head that he was now neither hungry nor thirsty. And yet to repeat a pleasure so intense and almost so spiritual seemed an obvious thing to do. His reason, or what we commonly take to be reason in our own world, was all in favour of tasting this miracle again; the childlike innocence of fruit, the labours he had undergone, the uncertainty of the future, all seemed to commend the ac-

tion. Yet something seemed opposed to this "reason." It is difficult to suppose that this opposition came from desire, for what desire would turn from so much deliciousness? But for whatever cause, it appeared to him better not to taste again. Perhaps the experience had been so complete that repetition would be a vulgarity—like asking to hear the same symphony twice in a day.

Later Ransom, the space traveller and spiritual sojournor, reflects: "This itch to have things over again, as if life were a film that could be unrolled twice or even made to work backwards . . . was it possibly the root of all evil?"

Perhaps not the root of all evil; but it certainly is the itch that motivates the self-appeasing seeking of many adventures. The quest is always toward final solution. Moreover, it is toward a joy which may transcend individual sacrifice in the sense that things are, by virtue of a completion of the quest, well with the world.

Comic Fantasy

C.N. Manlove

C.N. Manlove of the University of Edinburgh is considered the foremost scholar and critic in the field of fantasy literature today. In books for both adults and children, Manlove has found that the subgenre of comic fantasy continues to thrive and break new ground. These books are both playful and grounded in the familiar. Their absurd elements are excessive, but there is an inherent logic in them that readers can identify. Although the impossible can happen, it appears credible within the logic of the fantasy world. In this manner much of the humor in comic fantasy is derived from the juxtaposition of the workings of the fictional world and the workings of the real world.

Comic or fantastical fantasy is a distinct subgenre of fantasy, only occasionally occurring together with its "serious" counterpart. George MacDonald writes, on the one hand, profound books such as *Phantastes* (1858), *At the Back of the North Wind* (1870), *The Princess and the Goblin* (1872), *Lilith* (1895), or the short stories "The Golden Key" (1867), "Cross-Purposes" (1867), or "Photogen and Nycteris" (1879), and on the other, the isolated sparkle of the punningly absurd "The Light Princess" (1864). The graver books may contain touches of humor: *The Princess and the Goblin* has a good sense of a child's eye-view of reality, but the main concern is spiritual, a process of self-development in a struggle against evil. The main distinction of "The Light Princess" is its creative wit: when the story becomes moral and the prince in love with the flippant and aeriform princess resolves to sacrifice himself to restore her to full humanity, a different note is present; the spiritual recovery of the princess involves her becoming heavy, and the story becomes "grave" with her. There is a similar contrast between the first book, *The*

Reprinted from "Comic Fantasy," by C.N. Manlove, *Extrapolation*, vol. 28, no. 1 (1987), pp. 37–43, with permission from The Kent State University Press.

Sword in the Stone, of T.H. White's *The Once and Future King* (1958), and the later books: in the first, while Arthur is young and his true identity unknown, there is much fun, whether in hunting, pursuing the wicked Morgan le Fay, or having very real lessons in zoology with the ludicrous Merlin. However, much of that is lost in the next, when Arthur is king and has to start thinking about how to stop wars. The comic fantasy exists mainly while Arthur is a child, without responsibilities. And much comic fantasy is written for children, such as Thackeray's *The Rose and the Ring* (1855), Dickens's "The Magic Fishbone" (1868), the *Alice* books (1865, 1872), Andrew Lang's *Prince Prigio* (1889) or *Prince Ricardo* (1893). Kenneth Grahame's "The Reluctant Dragon" (1898) or *The Wind in the Willows* (1908), E. Nesbit's *Five Children and It* (1902) or *Nine Unlikely Tales* (1901). A.A. Milne's *Pooh* books (1926,1928), and James Thurber's *The Thirteen Clocks* (1951) and *The Wonderful O* (1958).

There are exceptions to the points just made, of course. It is possible for the absurdities of comic fantasy to be fused with more serious purpose, as in Voltaire's *Candide* or Mervyn Peake's *Titus Groan* (but not his *Gormenghast* [1950], where the two impulses fall apart into divided sections of the book). There is comic fantasy for adults in such works as Shakespeare's *A Midsummer Night's Dream*, William Beckford's *Vathek* (1786), George Meredith's *The Shaving of Shagpat* (1856), and F. Anstey's *Vice Versa* (1882) or *The Tinted Venus* (1885). But comic fantasy for adults tends to the satiric, from Kafka's *Metamorphosis* (1916), Gogol's *The Nose* (1836), and the fantasies of James Branch Cabell to Mikhail Bulgakov's *The Master and Margarita* (1938). For a purely comic fantasy, the main interest in the story of *The Nose* would be the independent and grotesque existence of the nose itself as it parades about the streets of Petersburg, not its reflections of the vanity of its former owner, the worthy Collegiate Assessor Kovalev. Nor does comic fantasy of this sort have much to do with the uglinesses of life. In *Metamorphosis* Kafka is showing Gregor Samsa in a comic position, but the comedy becomes increasingly sordid as his beetledom becomes confirmed and he is rejected and finally dies in squalor. Satiric fantasy is referential, but comic fantasy tends not to be. Kafka's transformation of a man to a beetle is, in part, a satire on human self-importance (a beetle being in human eyes one of the lowest forms of life), but the transformations of a whole country's population to a bed of mussels in E. Nesbit's "Septimus Septimusson" *(The Magic World)* or of a king to "a villa-residence, replete with every modern improvement" in her "Cockatoucan" *(Nine Unlikely Tales)* are there simply for the sake of preposterous contrast.

PLAYFUL AND GROUNDED IN THE FAMILIAR

Serious fantasy may be said to be potentially "imaginative," in the sense that it often deals with spiritual issues and themes, where comic fantasy is "fanciful," in that it is concerned mainly with play. The difference can be presented as one between metaphysics and physics. The Phoenix that makes up one of the principles of creation in Charles Williams's *The Place of the Lion* (1931) is an expression of the divine, "momently consumed, momently reborn": but in E. Nesbit's *The Phoenix and the Carpet* (1904), it is a small, white-crested bird with perfect manners, considerable vanity, and remarkable fluency in both idiomatic English and polite French. Where Williams' phoenix is seen only indirectly as "something," Nesbit's bird is physically handled, even taken to a theater performance inside one of the children's coats, whence it emerges "crushed and dishevelled." In comedy's emphasis on the physical, it is remarkable how many objects are in comic as compared to serious fantasy, and how often comic fantasy resorts to lists, as though determined to cram in as much detail as possible, from the "beasts, birds, millstones, clocks, pumps, bootjacks, umbrellas, or other absurd shapes" into which Fairy Blackstick has transformed "numberless wicked people" in Thackeray's *The Rose and the Ring*, to the multiple constituents of E. Nesbit's Psammead or sand-fairy, an amalgam of spider, monkey, snail, bat, and pig, in *Five Children and It.* The identities of things in serious fantasy are often blurred at the edges, fading into the spiritual. Tolkien's Ents or hobbits or Lewis's planet Perelandra or his Un-man, solidly described though they may be, are in part spiritual existences, instinct with natural and supernatural good or evil. Identities in comic fantasy are hard-edged and definite; as Coleridge said of fancy, comic fantasy deals with "fixities and definites."

This lack of physical reality occurs in part because serious fantasy often deals with at least partly familiar images which are resonant with meaning. Hobbits may seem new, but their name conveys their nature: yokelish and rabbitish. Gandalf is a traditional wizard; T.H. White's Merlyn is not. The universe as C.S. Lewis portrays it in his Space Trilogy is reminiscent of the medieval cosmos, and the floating islands of Perelandra seem to draw Ransom with a "cord of longing . . . [that had] been fastened long long before his coming to Perelandra . . . before the origins of time." Much serious fantasy looks to the past for its values and creates worlds founded on medieval lines. But comic fantasy exploits the novel and the bizarre, from darning needles that can speak to flamingos used as croquet mallets or toads driving cars. (It is worth reflecting on how much of this is also the case with a poem such as Pope's *The Rape of the Lock*, which is usually considered only in terms of its serious moral intent.) To this may be added that comic fantasy often deals with miniature worlds involving the magnification of small objects: *The Rape of the Lock*, the tiny fairies of *A Midsummer Night's Dream*, the first two books of *Gulliver's Travels*, the vegetable gnomes of E.T.A. Hoffmann's "The King's Betrothed" (1821), the worlds of Hans Christian Andersen, Charles Kingsley's *The Water-Babies* (1863), *Alice, Pooh, The Wind in the Willows, The Sword in the Stone*, perhaps even Mary Norton's *The Borrowers* (1952). In serious fantasy, there is rather an expansion than a contraction of purview: whole worlds serve as background and the hero goes on a quest, as in the work of MacDonald, William Morris, David Lindsay, Lewis, Tolkien, White, and Ursula Le Guin; or the dimensions of a place expand, as in Peake's *Gormenghast*. Kingsley's *The Water-Babies*, being both comic and serious, both expands and contracts in that Tom shrinks to a waterbaby yet travels over all the world and finds it a far wider place than he had ever thought.

PARODY AND IRONY

Comic fantasy can depend for its effect on the collision of fixed opposites. One of the modes in which this occurs is parody, where the past and the traditional are lightly mocked (as they are not in serious fantasy) and turned into the absurd. One object of parody is the traditional fairy- or folk-tale. Many of E. Nesbit's shorter tales are founded on fairy-tale conventions, such as that by which fairy-godmothers must be invited to attend the christenings of royal infants to bestow magic blessings or curses: the fairy Malevola in

"Melisande" thrusts herself forward to pronounce that "'the Princess shall be bald'" (*Nine Unlikely Tales*). Nesbit's amalgam, the Psammead, is a reversal of the standard graceful fairy. *The Rose and the Ring*, "The Magic Fishbone," "The Reluctant Dragon," and *The Thirteen Clocks* are also parodies of traditional tales. The Harvard Lampoon's *Bored of the Rings* (1969) parodies Tolkien's *The Lord of the Rings* in Thurberesque style: "'The Shadow is growing and your journey is long. It is best to begin at once, in the night. The Enemy has eyes everywhere.' As he spoke, a large, hair-covered eyeball rolled ominously from its perch in a tree and fell to the ground with a heavy squelch." However, to be fully a comic fantasy, a parody ought to be self-contained: where the parodic intent is dominant, fantasy does not fully exist. The actions of the characters in *Bored of the Rings* would not be comprehensible without a knowledge of *The Lord of the Rings*, and the same might be said of the absurdities of Pope's *The Dunciad*, which only a knowledge of Virgil's *Aeneid* can place in a proper pattern, or of Hawthorne's "The Celestial Railroad" (1846) in relation to Bunyan's *Pilgrim's Progress*. The world of comic fantasy is able to stand on its own, as a comic creation *sui generis*, though obviously a knowledge of the parody present will help the fun, as in the references to the style of G.P.R. James in *The Rose and the Ring*. And in such fantasy the parody is in its own way nonreferential: it is not present simply to make a point about the literature parodied, as Fielding's *Shamela* does about Richardson's *Pamela*.

More generally comic fantasy involves clashes between serious and comic contexts. Comedy exists when a statue of Venus comes to life and becomes rudely enamored of an already-betrothed Victorian hairdresser in F. Anstey's *The Tinted Venus*. It exists when the children in E. Nesbit's *The Story of the Amulet* (1906) travel to the past and teach Julius Caesar how a cap pistol works or guide the Phoenician sea captain Pheles with a shilling compass, or are addressed thus by the Queen of Babylon when first she meets them, "'I really am so glad you came! . . . I was getting quite too dreadfully bored for anything!'" It is present even when moral laws are exuberantly flouted, as in Beckford's *Vathek* when the caliph uses the sacred besom brought from the Caaba of Mecca to sweep away spiders' webs, or when his mother Carathis "who never lost sight of her great object, which was to obtain favor with the powers of darkness, made select parties of the fairest and most delicate ladies of the city; but in the midst of their gaiety, she contrived to introduce vipers amongst them, and to break pots of scorpions under the table. They all bit to a wonder; and Carathis would have left her friends to die, were it not that, to fill up the time, she now and then amused herself in curing their wounds, with an excellent anodyne of her own invention; for this good princess abhorred being indolent." In every case the implied datum is some fixed norm against which the comedy plays, purely for fun.

JUXTAPOSING THE NORMAL AND THE ABSURD

Many other kinds of juxtaposition of opposites occur in comic fantasy. There are the limericks of Edward Lear, which seem to propose sense, only to fall into inconsequence in the last line. There is the looking-glass world of *Alice,* with the world upside-down or sense reversed. There is the inversion of values, whereby the trivial has become the important, as in *The Rape of the Lock;* or in another way, in Hoffmann's "The King's Betrothed," where Fräulein Anna is wooed by a gnomish carrot. There is the interplay of logic with absurdity, particularly as used by E. Nesbit and by James Thurber: in the latter's *The Thirteen Clocks,* after having struggled in vain to shift the frozen hands of the clock by touching them, the Golux concludes, correctly, "'If you can touch the clocks and never start them, then you can start the clocks and never touch them. That's logic, as I know and use it.'" This absurd logic can be seen too in Calvino's *The Cloven Viscount* (1951), where the half-viscount who falls in love with the peasant girl Pamela leaves the evidence of his affection in the form of fields of daisies, parsnip blossoms, and dandelion flowers with half their petals stripped off. Or there is the collision of fantastic rules with reality, as in E. Nesbit's *Five Children and It,* in which one of the rules of each magic wish granted by the Psammead is that its results will be evident to none but the children, so that when on one occasion they accidentally wish that their baby brother "the Lamb" were grown up, and he is, into a languid young man called Hilary Devereux, the nursemaid Martha is unable to perceive the change and picks Hilary up as though he were still a two-year-old:

> The grown-up Lamb (whose names shall now be buried in oblivion) struggled furiously. An expression of intense horror

and annoyance was seen on his face. But Martha was stronger than he. She lifted him up and carried him into the house. None of the children will ever forget that picture. The neat grey-flannel-suited grown-up young man with the green tie and the little black moustache—fortunately, he was slightly built, and not tall—struggling in the sturdy arms of Martha, who bore him away helpless, imploring him, as she went, to be a good boy now, and come and have his nice brem-milk!

The antagonisms of comic fantasy are different from those of serious fantasy, where the opposition is most frequently one between good and evil: in comic fantasy the interplay is always between some kind of norm and an absurdity. This could be said of much comedy, but comic fantasy carries the disparity to extremes. And if serious fantasy would often propose that evil is a shadow, a nonentity to be overcome, comic fantasy is much more dialectical, requiring both of its sides to exist to provide the arcing that gives it life. And that life is at its most potent the more absurd the comedy becomes. In *Vathek* the conflict between the grotesque crimes of the caliph and the moral laws which eventually quite literally constrain him give the work its life. In Voltaire's *Candide* the ludicrous exuberance with which the hideous violences done on the characters and the persistently optimistic philosophy of Pangloss are recounted supply the humor. In *Winnie-the-Pooh* A.A. Milne can use the notion of a wise owl (still believed to be wise by the other animals) to give us a stupid bird who cannot even read his name. In *A Midsummer Night's Dream* Titania becomes by magic besotted with an ass. In E. Nesbit's "The Princess and the Hedgepig," the princess is told that she will be banished from her kingdom until she can find " 'a thousand spears to follow her to battle' "; a prince preposterously enchanted to a hedgehog provides the solution with his thousand spines. In *The Rose and the Ring* the victory in battle of Prince Giglio is made certain by his possession of armour which is "waterproof, gun-proof, and sword-proof," and of a sword so prodigiously extensible that it can run through "a whole regiment of enemies at once."

The humor of comic fantasy lies nearer the preposterous than the simply amusing—that in part is its fantastic element. It is extreme humor, containing violent inversion. To that extent it is fitting that many of the people in it should be out of control, or given to excess, such as Titania, Vathek,

MacDonald's light princess, the Queen of Hearts in *Alice,* Toad in *The Wind in the Willows,* Bulgakov's maniacal cat-devil Behemoth, Calvino's savage half-viscount, or the foaming Duke in Thurber's *The Thirteen Clocks.* To some extent what comic fantasy portrays is the eventual neutralization of that excess—the disabusing of Titania, the infernal constraint on Vathek, the acquired gravity of the light princess, the reduction of the Queen of Hearts to a playing card, the repentance of Toad, the departure of Behemoth, the reunifying of the cloven viscount, the overthrow of the Duke. A central motif—it can hardly be called a theme—of comic fantasy is the struggle between control and freedom, from the conflict of human wishes and limiting magic rules in E. Nesbit's work to the interplay of sense and nonsense in *Alice* and morality and immorality in *Vathek.* The life of the comedy and the fantasy exists so long as those opposites are in tension, even if the eventual resolution in a return to the sensible, controlled and moral order is desired.

CREATING JOY FROM THE IMAGINATION

The world of comic fantasy is frail. Often it is made part of a child's world only. Christopher Robin grows out of it. Alice dreams it. It is a construct that does not ask more than temporary acceptance of its laws. Serious fantasy invites some measure of belief, or at least what Tolkien has called Secondary Belief. This is particularly true of Christian fantasy, and readers are expected to feel the reality of all such worlds—Middle-earth, Arcturus, Gormenghast, Gramarye, Earthsea—while reading them. But comic fantasy exist arbitrarily: it is a thing that should not be but is; it dances always on the edge of its own nonentity. Readers know that Vathek's realm never was, that there is no Pantouflia, no Psammead, no Golux; these things have no roots in our reality. Given the sorts of chaos that they cause it is not always wishful that they did. All that comic fantasy says is "Let's pretend." That pretence is its whole basis. Comic fantasy is always aware of norms and how its world diverges from them—how a fairy traditionally should look, how people normally behave, what rules are like in real life, how magic disguises reality: it depends for its existence on the knowledge that the actions and worlds it portrays are contingent. Serious fantasy is not so concerned with its violations of norms. Often it ignores reality and standards altogether, as in Peake's Gormenghast books or Ursula Le Guin's Earthsea books, which create worlds without reference to this one. Or it shows that contemporary norms and views of reality are inadequate: C.S. Lewis, in his Space Trilogy, tries to show how the universe may be far richer than supposed, and Charles Williams does the same for the Earth in his novels; George MacDonald portrays the empirical view of existence as insufficient. But comic fantasy always looks over its shoulder to an outer reality or standard for its effects. Its central impulse is a delight in playful creation. It says, "We know there is no such world as the one I shall present, yet I shall present it." It directs readers to its own creativity, its wit, its ingenuity. The final juxtaposition of opposites on which comic fantasy depends is that between "is" and "is not." Toys cannot speak, nor dormice attend tea-parties, and there is no Eeyore: and yet this certainty is continually played against by the solidity with which these creatures are imagined. "'People come and go in this Forest, and they say, 'It's only Eeyore, so it doesn't count.' They walk to and fro saying 'Ha ha!' But do they know anything about A? They don't. It's just three sticks to *them*.'" Comic fantasy always direct readers to its being and to the being of its inhabitants: it is fundamentally ontological in its concern.

The delight of comic fantasy is in making the impossible happen, in creating an absurd world that is held together by its own internal laws once the initial assumptions are made. The characters and happenings in the *Alice* books are absurd but at the same time are explicable in terms of the laws of reversal. There are always two elements in comic fantasy: the mind at its freest, creating the most bizarre creatures and events, and a controlling and governing medium in which these events are set and which gives them a temporary point and interconnection. That is the desire at the heart of comic fantasy—to let the imagination go quite wild and yet at the same time make that wildness appear inevitable and credible. It is between those two points that the metaphoric life of the genre is struck.

Characterization in Tolkien's *Lord of the Rings*

Dwayne Thorpe

Dwayne Thorpe, a professor of English at Washington and Jefferson College, believes that the characters in fantasy fiction are drawn differently than in other genres. Fantasy characters are stereotypes fulfilling recognizable roles in a story line. But the best fantasy writers are able to reveal through their characters the complexity of themes in their work. This adds depth to the characters and allows them to be more than mere caricatures of good and evil. Thorpe uses Tolkien's *Lord of the Rings* to illustrate how a writer of fantasy needs to create well-rounded characters, while keeping in mind that they must be archetypal.

To a realist, Tolkien's characters are clearly stereotypes. But Tolkien's readers are incensed by the assertion. Gandalf may wear a pointy hat and hurl fireballs, but he is, they feel, as intensely real as [Dostoevsky's] Raskolnikov. The disagreement does not spring from the ill-will of realists or the bad faith of fantasy readers, but from the attempt to apply the concepts of realism where they are inappropriate. It is quite right to say that Gandalf has only two dimensions, the Grey and the White. But it is quite wrong to call him a caricature, because in fantasy terms like "stereotype" and "caricature" have no meaning. These are categories of realism.

CREATING ROUNDED CHARACTERS

Methods of characterization are functions of the entire design and purpose of literary works. Because realism is mimetic, based on the concept of the mirror, its strongest impulse is to make characters seem three-dimensional, as if

Excerpted from "Fantasy Characterization: The Example of Tolkien," by Dwayne Thorpe, *Mythlore*, Summer 1991. Reprinted with permission from the author.

they belonged in the world outside the text. It therefore values nuance above all things and pursues it in two modes: *external,* mimicking observed behavior, and *internal,* mimicking the flow of thought.

Henry James, a masterful practitioner of the first mode, achieves the illusion of reality by paying close attention to surfaces. In a typical passage, one of his characters, Daisy Miller, shifts between saying "he doesn't" and "he don't" four times within a single page. James calls no special attention to these shifts—they can be and are regularly missed—but leaves the reader to see for himself and draw his own conclusion. If we miss that detail, we will surely see others, for "Daisy Miller" is built on dozens of such nuances—a technique that mimics experience, where trivial details frequently reveal character and we must sort out impressions without the aid of an author.

James Joyce on the other hand, practicing internal realism, uses stream of consciousness. Here is Stephen Dedalus walking along the strand in *Ulysses,* Joyce's technique convincingly imitating the mind's associative leaps:

> Yes, evening will find itself in me, without me. All days make their end. By the way when next is it Tuesday will be the longest day. Of all the glad new year, mother, the rum tum tiddledy tum. Lawn Tennyson, gentleman poet. *Gia.* For the old hag with the yellow teeth. And Monsieur Drumont, gentleman journalist. Gia. My teeth are very bad.

The techniques are "opposites" in some ways, but both kinds of realism, external and internal, are designed to convince the reader that they mirror reality. But other narratives have other work to do. Characters in didactic literature, for instance, illustrate ethics. The parable of the Prodigal Son teaches not how people live but how they *should* live. It would be as improper to provide detailed descriptions of the prodigal's clothing or stream of consciousness as it would be to intrude a comment on proper grammar in *Daisy Miller:* an impropriety one feels in the DeMille-inspired biblical extravaganzas, which give us accurate costumes rather than incisive wisdom. Didactic characterization should provide not three-dimensional facts but moral depth.

Three-dimensional characterization has no more value in fantasy than in parable, for fantasy provides not character development but dreams and nightmares. To the extent that the writer has brought these to life, the fantasy does its work. . . .

However, having said as much, I must add an important

qualification. While the tools of the realist, the moralist and the fantasist are not and cannot be the same, fantasy no more exists in an autonomous world than other works do. It is illegitimate to demand that a fantasy follow the "rules" of the realistic novel, but it must meet the test of all art: the test of depth. A realistic story may be thoroughly realistic and still fail by being trivial, as the once-numerous "slice of life" stories proved by fading into literary history. A didactic tale may oversimplify the moral questions it deals with, as Parson Weems' little fiction about Washington demonstrates. And fantasy may offer shallow dreams: pornography, carnography, propaganda, coy fancies. Good fantasy, on the other hand, is adequate to the desires and fears it evokes. . . .

It is clear that Tolkien's tale has entertained millions of readers. But the critic must consider the implications of their delight. Does the thread of consistency which runs through Middle-earth match the truth of the human heart? Does it satisfy primordial desires? Or is there something childish about it? Those who love the work, wishing to distinguish it from stories with little more than plot lines, have often said that *The Lord of the Rings* contains an important moral point: the triumph of good over evil. In a way the work is didactic, of course, as the destruction of Sauron demonstrates. But one would have thought the long stretch of pages—more than a hundred of them—which follows Sauron's defeat adequately demonstrates that his destruction is not the main point. . . . A writer bent on showing the triumph of good over evil would be well-advised to at least keep them separate. But Tolkien does not. The motives of characters like Boromir, for instance, present us with puzzles in ethics. Good has its unexpected complications. Gandalf is the champion of good, but his genuine fear of losing, his death in Moria, his fear of taking the ring, his rudeness—all these are bones to sharpen one's ethical teeth on. Of course there is moral depth in the portrait: the sad truth about goodness, as it were. But *The Lord of the Rings*, although it contains prominent didactic elements, is not a didactic work. We come closer to its center through its oddities.

DETAILS CREATE CHARACTER TYPES

One of these is the remarkable fact that there are no graves in the Shire. Yet, just outside its borders the world is filled with grave mounds and memorials to the dead: the Barrow

Downs; the ancient defensive walls around Weathertop; the pillars of the Argonath; the Dead Marshes; the burial mounds of Rohan. The explanation is to be found in the function of the Shire. On a personal level, the Shire, where an eleventy-first birthday is possible, fulfills what Tolkien called "the oldest and deepest desire, the Great Escape: the Escape from Death." But it also works on a cultural level, as a fantasy of stability in a century of change and destruction: a rural world, sufficient to itself, untouched by the machines of Saruman, which [Tolkien asserts] allows the reader to escape "the rawness and ugliness of modern European life." *The Fellowship of the Ring* structurally repeats and magnifies that escape, bringing us to Lothlorien, a magnified Shire: a forest of mallorns where the very houses are in trees; where the pavilion pitched around Bilbo's birthday tree has grown to Cerin Amroth, "the heart of the ancient realm as it was long ago"; where winter flowers bloom forever "in the unfading grass: the yellow *elanor,* and the pale *niphredil.*" Here conservative ways yield to the changeless, and hobbits give way to elves.

Other oddities are harder to explain but just as important: for instance, the transformation of Strider into Aragorn, Aragorn into Elessar, and Elessar into the heir of Elendil. As the names change, so does the person, even in appearance, from a disreputable-looking vagabond to a seasoned friend of Gandalf, then to a man intimate with elves, and finally to the returning king with healing hands. It is not character development but radical change which takes us from the *Prancing Pony* to the Pillars of the Argonath, where Aragorn beneath the statues of Isildur and Anarion calms the frightened hobbits. "Fear not! . . . Under their shadow Elessar, the Elfstone, son of Arathorn of the House of Valandil, Isildur's son, heir of Elendil, has nought to dread!" (I, "The Great River").

As the king ascends into his titles, we see a unique approach to characterization. Realistic literature has been dominated by the idea of the individual, but Tolkien emphasizes those qualities which make a character representative, not unique. His characters are not products of an internal dynamic. They are rarely even self-reflective and have nothing which could properly be called interior lives. One cannot imagine analyzing Gandalf's psychology—or Frodo's—for this is a book without autonomous individuals.

This approach to characterization is no flaw but part of

Tolkien's imaginative consistency. The dream of a world which transcends time demands characters equal to splendor, not subject to eccentricity. It also demands that the reader be made adequate to the characters. Tolkien's methods consistently aim to produce both results. Here, for instance, is the introduction of Boromir. "Seated a little apart was a tall man with a fair and noble face, dark-haired and grey-eyed, proud and stern of glance" (I, "The Council of Elrond"). Tolkien does not use striking details, which would turn the reader's attention to matters of fact. Instead, he establishes a matrix of adjectives which elevate the reader to the position of unerring judge. We do not struggle to understand Boromir. We begin by understanding him.

The pitfalls of such a method are obvious. The author, having announced in advance what we are to think, is free to flout standards. He can declare splendor while producing frippery, set up poses instead of heroes, and cultivate rhetoric rather than learn honest style. Tolkien's imitators have in fact fallen into all these traps. But Tolkien, I think, does not. The details of Boromir's physical appearance which immediately follow his introduction are an example.

> He was cloaked and booted as if for a journey on horseback; and indeed though his garments were rich, and his cloak was lined with fur, they were stained with long travel. He had a collar of silver in which a single white stone was set; his locks were shorn about his shoulders. On a baldric he wore a great horn tipped with silver that now was laid upon his knees.

What kind of man wears rich clothing on such a journey? The fine clothes, the jewelry, the striking appearance, in another work would indicate the hero: Prince Valiant or his equivalent. Here, they play a very different role, introducing a man who believes in his own superiority. The true hero, an undistinguished hobbit, has already been introduced. All the traditional heroes gathered here—the wizard, the warrior, the king in exile—are in fact secondary. In the scene that follows, Boromir, the heroic patriot, reveals his limits and lays the groundwork for his failure, the real end toward which Tolkien is moving. Why has *Boromir* come in response to *Faramir's* dream? Why does he deprecate and doubt all strength and knowledge but his own, when it is clear that he needs help both to interpret the dream and to withstand the strength of Mordor? His misguided trust in himself implies an equally wrong distrust of others: a distrust which surfaces when he doubts Aragorn's claim to the throne and climaxes when his desire for the Ring's power overcomes his loyalty to its bearer. The horn on his knees, like the bow of Odysseus, is one of those objects in heroic literature which embody the character of their masters. And when Boromir interrupts the order of speakers, usurping Elrond's place in his own house, boasts of his deeds, and insists (despite the need for secrecy) on sounding the horn before he sets out, the alert reader may well remember what is meant by "blowing one's own horn."

DISTINGUISHING CHARACTERS THROUGH SPEECH

Though a reader who expects stereotypes may fail to see it, nothing in this description is simple ornament. Each detail challenges expectation. The same is true of Boromir's speech. All Tolkien's characters speak unrealistically, of course. But they are not all of a piece. Their range encompasses Elrond's archaic nobility; Grima Wormtongue's ugly sounds and images; Sam's inimitable hobbitese, Saruman's twentieth-century political rhetoric; and Aragorn's simple gravity. Taken together, these speakers present a world in which each tongue plays its part. In Middle-earth, as a character speaks, so he is, and Boromir's use of words marks him clearly. He begins:

> Give me leave, Master Elrond, first to say more of Gondor; for verily from the land of Gondor I am come. And it would be well for all to know what passes there. For few, I deem, know of our deeds, and therefore guess little of their peril, if we should fail at last.

Here is all the inflated rhetoric which the realist, suspicious of grandeur, anticipates and condemns: inverted phrases; alliteration; archaic words; parallelisms with more rhythm than information. But no other Tolkien character speaks quite that way. Boromir's wooden rhetoric points up the flaw in his makeup—it is a part of the consistency of his character—and the implied doubt of the conventional concept of the hero is confirmed in his fate. There is supreme irony when he, at Amon Hen, the Hill of Sight, blinded by his obsession with Gondor, assaults the ring bearer, betrays his own ideals, and dies.

This dissection of a heroic type must be taken seriously in a fantasy, where the celebration of heroes is the usual order of the day. Yet Tolkien is not being satirical nor deflating the idea of the warrior. Boromir in fact performs heroically and even in failure redeems himself through the manner of his death. Moreover, his replacement is hardly better. Frodo has no special strength, talent or intelligence—does not even know where he is going unless someone points him in the right direction. He can only keep putting one foot in front of the other. In the end, he cannot even do that. Having reached his goal, he fails completely and claims the ring as his own. If the traditional heroes have been replaced by a new one, why is the new one no better?

THE HERO CANNOT BE PERFECT

Carolyn Caywood, a columnist for the School Library Journal, *believes that not only must heroes have worthy adversaries, they must have weaknesses, too.*

If villains need to be vague then heroes must be human, wrestling with the sacrifices they have to make or trying to ease tensions between the various peoples they represent. It is primarily this interaction between those on the side of good, rather than with their opponents, that allows the heroes to change and grow. This interaction also can be used for comic relief, without which the dualism of good and evil slides into preachiness. . . .

One element of characterization that can trip up authors and their heroes is predestination. In a supernatural showdown, prophecy can heighten suspense and foreshadowing, but to be effective it must be cryptic and murky. Even more important, it must not drive the character, because that drives out characterization. Heroes who can't lose aren't very heroic, and those who never question whether they're up to the challenge or on the right course have no validity in teens' lives. In fact, heroes like these can come to resemble their adversaries if they don't have a measure of human frailty. . . . In the long run, it's a hero's weakness, inexperience, fear, and occasional foolishness that convince readers they too can confront seemingly overwhelming odds.

Carolyn Caywood, "The Quest for Character," *School Library Journal*, vol. 41, no. 3, March 1995, p. 152.

In the midst of this list of oddities, the strangest fact of all is that these failures are not failures but disguised triumphs. When Boromir assaults Frodo and dies protecting Merry and Pippin, there is no tragedy. He simply drives Frodo and

Sam east with the Ring while Sauron and Saruman are dis-
tracted by the wrong hobbits. His "failure," then, makes the
victory over Sauron possible. In the same way, Frodo's "failure" makes it possible for Smeagol to take a wholly unantic-
ipated but perfect part in the victory. One thinks of the Music of the Ainur, that irresistible harmony which makes
Tolkien's universe a *concors discordia,* and of which *The
Lord of the Rings* is the chief illustration. . . .

AVOIDING STEREOTYPES AND OTHER PITFALLS

But Tolkien's fantasy world does not just satisfy a primordial
longing. Following "the truth of the human heart" means
more than providing pleasant dreams. The author of a great
fantasy dramatizes the complexity of our desires. If the consistency of a fantasy world depends upon falsifying or omit-
ting that complexity, then its consistency really does sink to
the level of stereotypes and caricatures. Many fantasies do
precisely that. Their worlds, as a consequence, can easily be
divided into traps and happiness machines. But Middle-
earth derives immense power from being neither. Like the
fate of Boromir, which contains victory within the bitterness
of defeat, Middle-earth is a happiness machine disguised as
a trap. Only at the end is the disguise whisked away, when
the inhabitants of the East, the land of graves, are drawn into
the Shire and beyond, to the Undying Lands. This mixing of
elements is the chief means by which Tolkien creates a fantasy at once brighter and more brooding than most: one
which cleaves to "the truth of the human heart"—not just
the truth of our longings but also of their implications.
Though this is a fantasy of escape from death and of stability, those very yearnings are probed with an honesty equivalent to Hawthorne's. These same yearnings caused Sauron
to create the One Ring, drove Boromir to attack Frodo, and
destroyed the Numenorean kings. "Death was ever present,"
Faramir relates, "because the Numenoreans still, as they
had in their old kingdom, and so lost it, hungered after endless life unchanging" (II, "The Window on the West"). Even
Frodo is not exempt. How is he different from Sauron when
he uses the threat of the Precious to bend Gollum to his will?
How is he different from Boromir if, at Mount Doom, he replays Boromir's failure at Amon Hen? In his defeat and
heroic self-sacrifice, where pride and heroism are absolutely intertwined, Boromir reveals the complex truth of

our longings: the truth of the human heart. His dilemma lies at the center of *The Lord of the Rings*. I do not mean to suggest that this is his story, or that his fate holds some hitherto unseen key to the meaning of it. I am arguing, rather, that because it is a consistently imagined work—that is, a genuine work of art—all elements of *The Lord of the Rings*, even the smallest, radiate from its central issues. I have chosen to concentrate on Boromir, in fact, precisely because he is the least important of the tale's major characters.

IDENTIFYING AND EMPATHIZING WITH THE CHARACTERS

The ambiguous longings of Tolkien's characters are no different from our own, and Tolkien's greatest strength may lie in his understanding that primordial desire and fear are two sides of one coin. The reader's desire for the Undying Lands is also the desire of Sauron, who is frightening because he is a nightmare of ourselves: a searching eye which may see and take us. The relationship between undying elves and undead Nazgul ought to trouble us. So should the link which connects the ring-bearers, Frodo, Gollum, and Sauron. The book is filled with symmetries that point to the unity of our fears and desires. The ageless Tom Bombadil and the unsleeping barrow wight, Boromir and Faramir, Theoden and Denethor, whose very names are anagrams of each other, have a relationship which the reader feels, even when he cannot explain it. The fate of the Ring-bearer is sometimes misread by those who mistakenly see the One Ring as a symbol of power and trivialize Frodo's fate as the loss of a finger. But the One Ring is something very different, and the true sacrifice of Frodo is that, having suffered to save the Shire, he can no longer feel its satisfactions, The wound— "the memory of the burden," as Arwen calls it when she gives Frodo her place in the ship bound for the West (III, "Many Partings")—makes the Shire intolerable, and Frodo must leave it. Why? The power which makes the Ring both dangerous and irresistible, and which finally renders its bearer, no matter who he may be, unable to live with the world, is its gift of immortality. That gift has a price. Though fairy stories have often treated the desire for immortality, Tolkien adds that some of them rise above that level. *The Lord of the Rings* is one of those.

Most readers can easily see, I suppose, that the hobbits leaving the Shire in Book I are both themselves and embodiments of ourselves entering fantasy; and it is important that they go with both zest and regret: going to see elves but doomed, like Aragorn, to ride the paths of the dead. The road to the Undying Lands passes death and lamentation at every turn. In Rohan it passes through burial mounds blooming with Evermind, pulling us, by symmetries, back to the Barrow Downs, so similar to the mounds around Meduseld, but so much older that no one remembers why they are there. No Evermind grows on them, and the hunger of the barrow wight for departed life and wealth is terrifying. Why? We know, though we do not often say. "I am wounded," Frodo cries. "It will never really heal" (III, "The Grey Havens"). And we know, in the truth of our hearts, what wound that is. Frodo's wound, delivered by the undead, is no rip in the flesh. It is the yearning for immortality, for which there is no cure, in him or us. The counting of years, the close attention to the calendar, the desire for appendices and chronologies after the tale is done: these will not go away. Only the consolation of enchantment assuages us.

> *Faerie* contains many things besides elves and fays, and besides dwarfs, witches, trolls, giants, or dragons: it holds the seas, the sun, the moon, the sky; and the earth and all things that are in it: tree and bird, water and stone, wine and bread, and ourselves, mortal men, when we are enchanted.

So Tolkien wrote in defining fairy-stories. To be enchanted literally means to be brought inside a song. It is the highest ambition of Tolkien's characters. It is what Sam believes he has reached in Lothlorien and what he desires when he believes all is ended at Mount Doom. It was also, I believe, the highest ambition of the author of the tale. Something in the human spirit stands above alteration, lifting Tolkien's characters above the status of "individuals." Frodo's growth does not end at Mount Doom but in his journey through the dark, accompanied by the passing spirits of magic, to the Grey Havens, in a departure which is more than joyous or sad. It is one of the rare moments in the literature of this century to illustrate the full force of the word "solemn." As Tolkien gathers his strands together, drawing everything into that last scene, the symmetries of the work take the reader beyond questions of happiness and sorrow. In the solemn declaration that this is final—in the contrasting experiences of Frodo beholding the white shores and Sam beholding a shadow on the grey sea—characters and reader both come to see the pattern of the whole. We rise toward the level of the novelist, become conscious of the fiction, and escape, wakening as the dream ends.

It is one of Tolkien's gifts to show us the trap, allowing us to elude it. He wrote his son Christopher in December 1944, "If lit. teaches us anything at all, it is this: that we have in us an eternal element, free from care and fear, which can survey the things that in 'life' we call evil with serenity . . . without any disturbance of our spiritual equilibrium." The ending of *The Lord of the Rings* has sometimes been denigrated, but that seems to me wrong. Tolkien could have ended with something sonorous, but I am glad he did not. It is no mistake, but a deft final stroke, that as they take the East Road to Buckland at the end, Merry and Pippin are already singing, and even the devoted Sam ends with, "Well, I'm back."

Robert Jordan and the Longing for a Premodern Past

Edward Rothstein

For the past decade Edward Rothstein, cultural critic
for *The New York Times,* has closely tracked the popularity of Robert Jordan's fantasy series The Wheel
of Time. Considered by many the true heir of J.R.R.
Tolkien, Jordan's epic works put him in a league all
his own. Within his best-selling volumes Jordan creates an extensive pastoral world threatened by great
evil. To Rothstein this seemingly overused fantasy
setting is adopted by Jordan and other twentieth-
century fantasy authors because it symbolizes a
longed-for era of human history that was untouched
by the evils of modern times.

When matters begin to look bleak for the weary wanderers
of J.R.R. Tolkien's "Lord of the Rings," they rest briefly in
Lothlórien, an Elven forest of surpassing beauty. The river
Nimrodel's cold waters seem to cleanse the soul, trees stand
with nearly immeasurable grandeur and in the fragrant
grasses grow flowers whose very names—elanor and
niphredil—seem to speak of grace and sweetness.

For a reader who knows how many trials are yet to come,
there is a poignancy to the sheltered forest's beauty; It is ancient and timeless, but also doomed. Even before the Dark
Power's evil, spreading outward from Mordor, can turn
Lothlórien's green leaves brown, the verdant land is colored
by the melancholy of last days. And when, laden with Elven
gifts, the travelers set off into the harsh, unsheltered landscape beyond the forest's borders, they gaze back, knowing
it will be seen no more by mortal being.

But what neither they nor their creator could have

guessed is that some version of Lothlórien would be revisited, re-created and reproduced by succeeding generations of adventurers, or that Tolkien's mid-20th-century vision of Paradise lost and Reality gained, with its wizardry, elves, orcs, lost kingdoms, dwarfs and epic battles, would itself come to haunt the world like a lost Lothlórien. The trilogy, along with Tolkien's prelude, "The Hobbit," was boosted into cultdom by the counterculture of the 1960's; since then, scores of epigones have spawned the genre of fantasy fiction.

Its entries now can be seen crowding long aisles in bookstores, thousand-page volumes straining the technology of paperback binding, their jackets decorated with gleaming swords and red cloaks, dragons exhaling fire, horse-drawn carriages, wizards' orbs, battles between half-human creatures and armored warriors. "At last, a worthy successor to Tolkien," a publisher's overheated proclamation might read. A recent anthology of fantasy fiction was called, "After the King: Stories in Honor of J.R.R. Tolkien." And every fantasy novelist does indeed yearn to be the King's heir.

These books are, like Tolkien's, multivolume epics, as if they were compilations of an alien culture's scripture, bearing subtitles like "Book 2 of the Malloreon" or "The Chronicles of Thomas Covenant the Unbeliever, Book 3." They promise esoteric knowledge and powers in their grand series titles: "Mage Storms," "Sword of Truth," "Keepers of the Hidden Ways." And they almost all require maps and glossaries to provide guidance in their often ornately designed worlds. In fact, Tolkien spawn have mutated and regenerated so much that now a simple hobbit with hairy toes—the hero of Tolkien's fantasy—would seem almost quaint. There are even fantasy role-playing games like "Dungeons and Dragons" and card games like "Magic: The Gathering" and the Tolkien-estate-licensed "Middle-Earth: The Wizards."

"THE WHEEL OF TIME" KEEPS TURNING

But now there really may be an heir of sorts to Tolkien, in attention earned if not achievement: Robert Jordan. In his saga, "The Wheel of Time," which began with "The Eye of the World" in 1990 and continued, most recently, with the seventh volume, "The Crown of Swords," which made it onto *The New York Times* best-seller list as soon as it was published last summer. Mr. Jordan has come to dominate the world Tolkien began to reveal. Five million copies of Mr. Jordan's books have been sold.

Mr. Jordan has created a universe so detailed that elaborate commentaries have developed on the Internet, news groups debate the fates of characters, sites on the World Wide Web attempt to foretell events looming in the promised eighth, ninth and tenth volume of this series. Even a reader with literary pretensions can be swept up in Mr. Jordan's narrative of magic, prophecy and battle. And given the author's almost effusive love of writing (according to the books' biographical note, he "intends to continue until they nail shut his coffin") and the meticulous plotting of each expansive volume, humankind may well reach its promised apocalypse before Mr. Jordan's characters do.

The thousands of pages written so far contain a multicultural compendium of peoples: a stern desert culture, a female priesthood, a serf society, a seafaring folk and governments of nobility and kings. There are small-town inns, castles and wind-driven boats. And through it all moves a messianic figure named Rand. An innocent young man, he is marked by prophecies as a figure around whom the forces of the age will battle. He is blessed—and cursed—with an unusual ability to "channel" a Power that has been strictly controlled by a female priesthood. That ability will, we are told, lead him to madness; he races against its temptations, trying to mold a political and military alliance that can join in a Last Battle against the Dark One and his minions. There are echoes of Christian and biblical iconography, allusions to the Arthurian legend and subtle invocations of other authors' fantasy worlds.

It may be unfair to Mr. Jordan to push the Tolkien comparison too far. Tolkien loved the sound and texture of language and invented one for his epic; he wanted the books to read like a translation from a lost Nordic tongue. His characters' bardic poems sound as if they had been passed on through generations, coding lost memories in song. And when he hits his truest notes, as he does when marking the passing of a glorious past, Tolkien can be heartbreaking. Mr. Jordan, though, is all dispatch; the narrative drive stops only to engage in minute description of a street, a battle, the feel of wielding the Power. There is a practical quality to these books—their job is to tell a story—and if sometimes the wheels of destiny turn a bit too noisily, and pasteboard romances become too overbearing, the pages still keep turning.

The Jordan books are indicative of how the Tolkien-inspired universe has changed since the 1940's, and of what the essence of its current appeal may be. After all, why should fantasy novels take place in societies that seem medieval? Why the thatched huts and stone castles, the hand-to-hand combat? Why the wizards and esoteric masters of magical power? And why has this become so distinctive a genre for the late 20th century?

ECHOES OF LOST WORLDS

Tolkien was a medieval scholar and philologist who had mastered Old English, Old Norse and Celtic languages, and he set himself the task of inventing not a literary genre but a lost language; that language would then provide the essence of a world, giving it its flavor, its myths, its conflicts. He wanted "The Lord of the Rings" to sound like a translation of a medieval epic romance originally written in a foreign tongue. Moreover, the spirit of the medieval romance, in Tolkien's case, also had a national significance, as the scholar Norman F. Cantor has shown. Tolkien fought in World War I and began writing his fantasies on the eve of World War II. Their world bears the marks of that experience and resonates with threats to England's heritage and the prospects of its decline.

Indeed, that world has already fallen before the books begin; it has already lost an ancient wisdom. It is full of ruins, allusions to lost powers, reminiscences of glorious kingdoms. But it is also on the brink of still greater disaster, in which Darkness threatens a final battle. A victory will not bring a restoration but will usher in a different age—a post-war universe—with new laws and pains.

This is almost exactly the situation in Robert Jordan's series. And Mr. Jordan's personal history in some ways seems an American echo of Tolkien's. Mr. Jordan, who lives in South Carolina, was educated at the Citadel and fought in Vietnam, earning the Distinguished Flying Cross and other honors. The books' battle scenes have the breathless urgency of firsthand experience, and the ambiguities in these novels—the evil laced into the forces of good, the dangers latent in any promised salvation, the sense of the unavoidable onslaught of unpredictable events—bear the marks of American national experience during the last three decades, just as the experience of the First World War and its aftermath gave its imprint to Tolkien's work. And Mr. Jordan also creates a world where a great deal of lore and knowledge is already forgotten and much that exists is badly scarred.

Tolkien and Mr. Jordan are not alone in their visions of postwar societies. The entire fantasy genre is preoccupied with the nature of nation-building and restoration, a subject that can seem far more central than the omnipresent magic and wizardry. In an often fascinating novel, "Tigana," by Guy Gavriel Kay, for example, the focus is on the plots and counterplots of political revolution and court confrontations. In a series of books about a Mormonesque prophet named Alvin Maker, Orson Scott Card attempts to provide an alternative history for the United States: folk magic is as real as the demonic forces hiding out in church, state and family. In her best-selling novel "The Mists of Avalon," Marion Zimmer Bradley draws on one of the touchstones of the fantasy genre—the Arthur legend—telling it from the point of view

---

JORDAN'S IMPACT ON HIS FANS

In an editorial in The New York Times, *Edward Rothstein discusses* The Wheel of Time's *effect on its devoted readers.*

"Wheel" draws on both [Jordan's] abstract knowledge and concrete experience; he creates a universe simple enough to master and then challenges the characters to do the same in meticulously choreographed battles against chaos and dissolution.

Meanwhile, readers have taken the challenge so seriously that there are some who, in New Agish devotion, think the books really are histories of alternative realities. In an interview, Mr. Jordan mentioned one Malaysian medical student who expressed a desire to abandon his training in order to become the author's spiritual disciple. He was swiftly discouraged.

But fantasy fiction, for all its artificial premises and cartoonish book jackets, is not as simple as it seems, nor is its audience. The 450 cognoscenti who turned out for Mr. Jordan's book signing at a Barnes & Noble were not easily classifiable by age. His publisher claims a broad spread of readers, and Mr. Jordan tells of a letter he received from an 88-year-old fan who urged him to write faster.

Edward Rothstein, "An Adored Fantasy Series Now Hints at 1990s Angst," *The New York Times*, October 26, 1998, p. 2.

of its women; at stake is the destiny of Britain.

There is also some resemblance to the popular 19th-century novel, which was often concerned with the origins of nations: Sir Walter Scott and Alexandre Dumas turned to Scottish legends and the French court for their wide-ranging tales. And, as in 19th-century novels, fantasy fiction attempts to show destiny unfolding on a large scale, describing societies from high to low, from king to peasant, from clan leader to serf.

TECHNOLOGY VS. MAGIC

It is odd that such attempts at realism should be combined with so thorough a determination to avoid earthly history. But that is part of the genre's point and goes along with its fascination with magic. Arthur C. Clarke once said that any sufficiently advanced technology is indistinguishable from magic, but although technology in fantasy might seem to be an invasion of alien forces, even Tolkien has one of his hobbits see a vision of what would become of his pastoral Shire should the battles against Evil be lost: the charming old mill is replaced by red-brick buildings belching black smoke.

This is familiar, too, from the world of 19th-century Romanticism. Technology creates division, darkness and unpredictable futures; magic binds and reaches backward to lost wisdom. Magic may be lost in the looming apocalypse, but in the meantime it is the source of the world's best hopes, its received wisdom as well as its inherited danger. So it should be no surprise that fantasy fiction often indulges in contemporary pop-religion or pop politics. The genre thrives in magazines called *Gnosis, Magical Blend, Renaissance* and *New Age.* Mr. Jordan's muscular tales rely on a notion of "channeling," and Ms. Bradley's vision of Camelot invokes druids, matriarchal goddess worship and astral travel. This is an odd genre, artificially ancient but almost always scented with the airs of contemporary New Ageism.

But fantasy fiction also is more somber than any New Age acolyte could be. New Age's messianism is sunny, expansive, promising an abundance of well-being. Fantasy is, at its best, somber, touched by melancholy and yearning. There is little question that after the great battles, after the apocalypse, after victory for the forces of good, the old order will begin to disintegrate: that is what happened to King Arthur's kingdom, to the Hobbit's Shire, and will probably doom Rand's world as well. Magic will fade, legends will pass; then will come the modern age we all know.

These books keep attempting to retell the story of our own pre-modern past, stripped of disease, poverty and hardship, blessed with villages and thatched huts. These early societies are already wounded, barely recollecting their own ancient heritage, and they struggle mightily against absolute Evil. But the genre's real twist is that victory itself is a defeat, for on the horizon are the forces of modernity itself. Then ordinary technology will arrive with its dark satanic mills. Nations will be formed. Earthly history will begin. And we will dwell within it.

Fantasy fiction takes place at the moment of imminent change, when all might be lost. It is medieval in atmosphere, 19th-century in its concerns, contemporary in its manners. It tells of old things anxiously clutched and new things barely formed. These novels are popular elegies at the edge of a new millennium, mourning for modernity, ersatz scriptures recounting our origins, reminding us again and again of the many Lothlóriens long gone, and the many battles yet to come.

CHAPTER 3

The State of the Genre Today

 Fantasy

Women Are Changing the Face of Fantasy

Charlotte Spivack

Charlotte Spivack is an authority on Arthurian fantasy and the author of *Merlin's Daughters,* a study of contemporary women writers of fantasy. She has found that women have modified and heavily influenced what was previously a male-dominated genre. Using a feminine perspective on plot, characters, and themes, they often subvert tradition story lines and present new value systems and new narrative forms to fantasy writing.

I must address the question of whether there is a distinctively feminine—or even feminist—fantasy or whether the top women writers of fantasy simply prove their ability to write superior versions of the traditional genre. I should also ask whether the genre itself is perhaps "feminine" as opposed to, at the extreme, hard-core "masculine" science fiction. . . .

FEMALE PROTAGONISTS

First let us look at the most obvious ways in which fantasy by female writers is different. The most immediately evident distinction is the choice of female protagonists. Andre Norton's Witch World series is about women; the trilogies of Ursula K. Le Guin and Patricia McKillip feature both female and male protagonists; Evangeline Walton, Vera Chapman, and Marion Zimmer Bradley all focus on female protagonists. Even more important than the mere choice of women as leading characters, however, is the concept of hero that underlies the choice. In much sword and sorcery written by women, for example, female heroes play conventional male roles as warriors. Their emphasis is on physical strength, courage, and aggressive behavior. In the fantasy novels the

Excerpted from *Merlin's Daughters: Contemporary Women Writers of Fantasy,* by Charlotte Spivack. Copyright © 1987 by Charlotte Spivack. Reproduced by permission of Greenwood Publishing Group, Inc., Westport, CT.

female protagonists also demonstrate physical courage and resourcefulness, but they are not committed to male goals. Whether warriors or wizards, and there are both, their aim is not power or domination, but rather self-fulfillment and protection of the community.

Furthermore, just as major women characters are often both masculine and feminine in their abilities, both expert with swords and devoted to peace, so male characters are also complex, with their aggressive natures modified by sensitivity. At the same time, those traditionally male traits of pride, sexual prowess, and desire for domination are often subjected to negative scrutiny. In short, the traditional roles of both men and women are reevaluated and recreated in these works. Probably the best examples of the modified male are found in the fantasies of Mary Stewart and Katharine Kurtz, which at first appear simply masculine in approach. Stewart's trilogy is devoted to the life of Merlin, the archetypal male wizard, but his intuitiveness, his sensitivity to nature, his minimizing of power, all seem feminine, permitting him in effect to function as the feminine side of his king. Kurtz's heroes in her two trilogies play traditional male roles, as warriors, priests, and politicians, but their conduct is by no means traditional. In her pseudomedieval fantasy world the male heroes exhibit traits usually associated with and often repressed as feminine.

A FEMININE PERSPECTIVE

Another overtly feminist strategy in these novels is the assumption of a female point of view on conventionally masculine subjects. Several women writers have turned to the Arthurian legend, which they have not dealt with in conventional ways. Instead, they offer a feminine perspective on the legendary events. Vera Chapman, for example, in her Arthurian trilogy, creates a new character to narrate part of the old story—King Arthur's daughter—and endows minor characters with strong personalities to narrate the rest—Bertilak's wife and Lynette. Both Marion Zimmer Bradley and Gillian Bradshaw retell events from the point of view of major female characters. Bradshaw makes Gwynhwyfar a first-person narrative voice, thereby reconceiving the role of the much maligned queen as a sympathetic woman. Bradley focuses on Morgan le Fay, recreating her role as a complex and positive character, far removed from the villainous part she plays in the original. Through these women narrators the events also shift in importance, with battles and politics losing emphasis in favor of human relationships and reactions.

A further narrative device favored by women fantasy writers is the circular as opposed to the linear plot. As Le Guin succinctly states it in her Earthsea trilogy, "To go is to return." Both Le Guin and Patricia McKillip in their trilogies put an emphasis on the second half of the traditional quest, the return, culminating in rebirth. The paradigm of the mythic hero, followed at least in part by most fantasists, includes eight stages from miraculous birth and inspired childhood through a period of meditation, the undertaking of a quest, a literal or symbolic death, journey to the underworld, and ultimately rebirth and apotheosis. Most, however, concentrate on the first half, with emphasis on the climactic nature of the quest. This heroic outward movement, responding to the call to adventure, is aimed at establishing the ego, as Joseph Campbell and others have pointed out, but the total self is not achieved until after the symbolic death, descent, and rebirth, followed by a return to the starting place. Le Guin's and McKillip's heroes return to their place of birth, as does Mary Stewart's Merlin, whose final enchanted sleep takes place in the very cave wherein he was conceived.

Another recurring feature in fantasy by women writers is the return to the matriarchal society of the ancient Celtic world. The traditional late medieval setting, with the panoply of chivalric knighthood, is rejected in favor of the very early or premedieval, before the worship of the goddess has given way to Christianity. The Grail as motif is thus often replaced by the sacred cauldron. Evangeline Walton's translation and adaptation of the Welsh epic *The Mabinogion* is a convincing depiction of life in ancient Dyved where the mother goddess was worshipped. Bradley also chooses a Celtic setting, with a plot stressing the conflict between the established matriarchy and the threatening new patriarchy introduced by Christianity. Andre Norton, on the other hand, creates her own original matriarchal society in her futuristic Witch World.

SUBVERSIVE MOTIFS

All of these techniques are clearly and readily apparent as feminist in focus: the emphasis on female protagonists, the preference for a matriarchal society as setting, the use of a circular rather than linear plot structure, and the assumption of a feminine point of view on subject matter traditionally presented from a male perspective. What more deeply distinguishes these fantasies by women writers is something much less obvious but ultimately much more significant. These works, which employ the fantasy quest as metaphor for the search for meaning through magic as metaphor for the transforming power of the creative imagination, are subtly but forcefully subversive of certain key concepts in the mainstream traditions of Western civilization. Much more than Tolkien, whose hobbits quietly prodded American youth into opposing the war in Vietnam, these fantasies are quietly undermining the foundations of capitalism, power politics, and Christian dualism. As Michael Butor points out in his study of the fairy tale, "[f]airyland is a criticism of ossified reality. It does not remain side by side with the latter; it reacts upon it; it suggests that we transform it, that we reinstate what is out of place." Similarly, in the secondary worlds of fantasy the wizard's spell and the dragon's flame are metaphorically endeavoring to transform society in the direction of feminist values.

The first of these subversive motifs is the renunciation of the power principle in politics. . . . Tolkien also introduces this theme but in a much more limited way. Frodo undertakes a quest to destroy the ring of power because the ring has been forged by a quintessentially evil figure. Power is the legitimate aim of other major figures representing the good. The aims of power-seeking are fulfilled in several ways that are positive in context: the dragon is slain, the war is fought and won, the king is restored to the throne. These goals are regarded as good ones. In contrast, in many of the fantasies written by women, the *desire* for power is denounced as a principle. It is not a matter of the good guys exerting power in order to crush the power-seeking of the bad guys. Instead, power-seeking as such is rejected. The goal in these quests is to *not* slay the dragon, to *not* take the treasure, to *not* seize the throne, to *not* dominate the Other.

In Andre Norton's Witch World, for example, the group of characters with potentially the greatest power is the Council of Witches. These gifted women have innate spiritual strength that enables them to perform magic. They use their skills in magic, however, only to negate or avert aggressive actions on the part of their power-hungry neighbors. The psychic power of these witches is superior to the steel weapons used by men. These wise women are committed to protecting their own free society and to maintaining the balance in nature. They use their magic to avert the threat of rape, war, and other forms of male domination, but when the threat is dispelled they do not establish their own political system. They retire to their own inner spiritual development. Their major antagonist is a technologically advanced society that they are forced to repel for the sake of remaining free. In so doing they do not adopt the technology that they see as a potentially dangerous base of tyrannical power.

Le Guin's Earthsea trilogy traces the career of a wizard from boyhood through maturity when he becomes an archmage. The major lesson he learns from his training is *not* to use the magical powers he possesses. Eager to perform impressive deeds of magic, he violates the stricture with disastrous consequences to himself and others. Through the course of the trilogy he gains maturity as he becomes able to manifest his wizardry through renouncing its usage except when absolutely necessary. He does not even kill the dragon but rather negotiates with it for future peaceful coexistence. The highest aim of wizardry is *being,* not *doing.*

The hero of McKillip's trilogy, *Riddle of the Stars,* is also faced with the challenge of accepting power, but he wishes to reject it from the start. The thoughtful, introspective type, he is part farmer, part student. His dearest wish is to marry his fiancée and settle down on his farm, spending his leisure in solving riddles, his favorite intellectual occupation. When he learns that it is his destiny to play an important role in the fate of the world, he desperately resists. Although the need to assume power is thrust upon him by the pressure of events, he never surrenders his desire for a quiet life of hard work and contemplation, without political involvement. He is by temperament what Le Guin's hero strives to become.

In her Arthurian trilogy, Gillian Bradshaw depicts the thrust for both military and political power as destructive of nature. More heroic than either the warriors or the leaders are the women who give birth, who heal, who suffer to maintain their families and households in the violent context of war and strife. Power comes and goes, passing through bloodstained hands, but the distaff world provides continuity through nurture. To the young mother whose husband is killed in battle the cause of empire is ill-conceived and meaningless. Even the death of King Arthur is shown to be the senseless result of a vain power struggle. What finally establishes Gawain as a member of the inner Arthurian circle is not his battle prowess, which he has demonstrated repeatedly to the point of madness, but rather his kindness to a fatally wounded soldier. Easing the pain of a dying man without any hope of reward or recognition is the highest kind of heroism. In feminist fantasy, then, power for the sake of power is denounced in favor of living and letting live. The code of the warrior and the ruler is deglorified and exposed as negative and destructive, while the role of the wizard is exalted for its perceptive passivity.

Rejecting Immortality

A second subversive theme in fantasies by women writers is the vindication of mortality. Contrary to accepted tradition, immortality, whether assumed as a literal afterlife or sought as a lasting fame in this life, is not aspired to. As Le Guin's hero explains [in *Farthest Shore*], "Death is the price we pay for our life." Her trilogy offers a vehement protest against a misguided desire for immortality. The concluding novel concerns the need to free Earthsea from the malignant influence of a sorcerer who has opened the gate between life and death in order to gain immortality for himself and, with it, power over others. All of the light, the color, and the joy have left the world since movement between life and death has become possible. Magic no longer works, for the loss of distinction has killed the imagination. The living exist in a shadowy way, resembling the world of the dead, the Dry Land, for without death, life has no meaning.

Susan Cooper's novels also incorporate the theme of rejecting immortality. She focuses on individual choice, presenting one character who opts for immortal life and one who refuses it. The unfortunate man who takes on the burden of immortality illustrates the dire consequences of everlasting life. He is a wanderer who has survived for centuries and longs to be freed from his endless existence. For him death will be a relief. The other character is a young man who discovers his identity as the son of King Arthur. Transposed to the modern age, he must choose between joining his legendary father in immortality or staying on the farm in Wales where he has been brought up by the rural couple whom he had thought were his parents. For him the immediate loving bonds of family are more important than the immortal role as Pendragon.

Evangeline Walton's handling of the same theme in her fantasy based on *The Mabinogion* shifts attention from the desire for immortality to the vindication of mortality. In the ancient Celtic world depicted in these works, desire for immortality on the part of an individual seems egoistically defiant of nature, for in the natural scheme of life all are reborn into higher levels of being. Death is therefore but a gateway to rebirth on a higher plane. The newly introduced Christian idea of eternal reward or punishment conflicts with belief in the goddess who claims both Time and Death as her children, and from whose womb will come rebirth as well as birth. The notion of an eternal afterlife imposes a moral structure on an inevitable natural process that is inherently evolutionary.

In dealing with Arthurian themes, both Bradshaw and Stewart stress acceptance of mortality in the context of the renewal of nature. Bradshaw's Gwynhwyfar will not accept the tale that Arthur will come again, preferring the consolation of spring, when life is naturally reborn. Stewart's Merlin retires to his cave, but not for an eternity.

DEPOLARIZATION OF VALUES

A third subversive theme is the depolarization of values. Nothing has been more central to fiction in the Western world than the depiction of conflict between right and wrong, hero and villain. The clarity and vehemence of the conflict have pervaded popular literature in particular, because of its generally diminished regard for moral and aesthetic ambiguity. But even allowing for the greater ambiguity inherent in major fiction, the lines of force are even there clearly drawn: [Dostoevsky's] Raskolnikov was wrong to murder the pawnbroker; [Dickens's] Scrooge should not have fired Bob Cratchett; [Twain's] Huck Finn was right to defend Jim, even at peril to his own soul. In the case of the women fantasy writers, however, these lines dissolve. One major example is the fiction of Le Guin, which is informed by Taoism in its moral structure. Unlike Christianity, Taoism rejects the polarization of opposites. Living well according to Taoism means living in harmony with nature, thereby maintaining a balance between natural opposites. In Earthsea good and evil do not exist as moral constructs, and light and dark are of equal value. Of the many elements held in binary suspension none is more basic than life and death, each of which requires the other.

In Norton's Witch World series, earthly standards of good and evil and moral judgments about reward and punishment become totally extrinsic and irrelevant on other planets. The hero of the first work is an army deserter in this world, but his humane sensitivity helps him become a savior in another. In McKillip's riddling world good and evil do not exist as concepts. By implication identity (more precisely, the search for identity) is valorized through the premium set on the ability to answer riddles, but truth remains the elusive ultimate riddle. In her narrative such modes of behavior as shape-changing function creatively or destructively, resisting ethical categorization. Furthermore, the omnipresent figure of Deth the harpist is both lauded and condemned, both accepted and rejected, emerging as a strong and essential presence but beyond moral judgment.

In the Arthurian and Celtic fantasies the depolarization of values is most evident in connection with sexuality. In the works of both Walton and Bradley sexuality is regarded as natural and blameless. In the absence of concepts of marriage, paternity, and legitimacy, the sexual act is free and fertility welcome. Sexual union is regarded as initiatory rather than possessive. Even incest is not prohibited, and Arthur's sense of guilt over the incestuous birth of Mordred is seen as a product of arbitrary Christian legalism.

In Bradshaw's Arthurian trilogy valorization is treated as a theme in itself. Her characters are concerned with the contrary forces of Dark and Light but find these opposites coexisting in every human being. Several who are devoted to serving the Light find themselves caught up in destructive behavior patterns that aid the Dark. Well-meaning characters perform actions that have negative consequences, but not out of malice or turpitude. Since things go both right and wrong in this world, moral blame is often essentially irrelevant. To condemn Gwynhwyfar's adultery as morally evil, then, is to misinterpret the act and misrepresent human reality.

The depolarization of values in feminist fantasy involves more than the rejection of moral dualism. One of the most profound and fundamental polarities is that of Self and Other. Much of human history has been characterized by political and religious intolerance of the Other. And in much literature male authors have posited the female as Other. Contrary to the long-established literary tradition of subduing or eliminating the Other as undesirable alien (or even of forcefully converting this alien presence, as in the case of Shylock), several women writers of fantasy direct their narratives toward acceptance of the Other, not merely dealienating it (and themselves) but actually integrating Self and Other.

Katharine Kurtz's double trilogy offers a striking illustration of this attitude. She is concerned with a gifted alien race, who are for centuries rejected as Other and mistreated for their giftedness. In these novels the perspective on discrimination is heightened through the fact that the difference—the Otherness—is one of superiority, not supposed inferiority. Fear motivates the prejudice of the establishment in the absence of any antisocial behavior on the part of those discriminated against. Andre Norton's novels concentrate on the integration of Otherness. In her elaborately imaginative other worlds, rational races exist in a multitude of forms. Wisdom of the scientific, philosophical, and mystical varieties exists in serpentine, winged, furred, and scaled as well as two-legged species. Similarly in McKillip's world, although the races are all human, the deeply engrained provincialism of the peoples from differing areas is unsullied by the aggressiveness of zenophobia. Otherness is an uncontested fact of life, a feature lending variety, amusement, and endless conversational possibilities.

Also implicit in depolarization is the rejection of transcendence in favor of immanence, a feature that sharply differentiates the fantasy worlds of the women writers from those of the Christian school, including the Inklings. One of the most elegantly detailed and pervasively immanent worlds is Le Guin's Earthsea. Although there is reference to a creator, clearly all is immanent within the creation. The highest wisdom available to the wizard is knowledge of the true names of things. These names are not imposed but derived, as the wizard finds Logos a process not unrelated to his own becoming. McKillip's world in its sly and subtle way is also an attack on transcendence. Much of her trilogy concerns the search for the so-called High One, who may or may not exist. Transcendence has been inherited in this world as an hypothesis but not wholly believed in and vulnerable to disproof. Here, as in Earthsea, understanding a thing is based on knowing its name, but here it is carried further to the point of transformation. Knowing about trees enables one ultimately to become a tree. Needless to say, tapping that deep-down sense of identity with trees in oneself is not easy.

SIMPLER SOCIETIES

Inherent in the theme of immanence is the stress on the importance of the natural environment. These fantasies are ecology-minded, often with an attendant bias against technology which is usually regarded as exploitative. Earthsea is totally without modern technology, and the heart of the ethical dictum is maintaining the balance in nature. In the Witch World, the enemies of nature as well as of human peace are the technological societies. In Walton's series the earth is worshipped as a manifestation of the mother goddess. To neglect the needs of the earth or to endanger its fruitfulness is to strike at the heart of life, all life. In Bradley's Celtic world the sacred places are those in nature. Worship must take place out of doors, not in a building, which is a human structure. Trees and waters are sacred. One social dimension of this attitude toward fecund nature is sexual permissiveness. Cutting down trees and prohibiting sex are both violations of nature.

In the fantasy fiction of contemporary women writers, then, certain patriarchal systems prevalent in our time are quietly being questioned, subverted, and revisioned. Far from being cute stories about unicorns written for juveniles, these mature, thought-provoking novels represent an intellectual and imaginative rebellion against the status quo. Through their prevailing metaphor of magic, they seek to transform society through the creative power of the imagination. The quest is a fantasy metaphor, but the transformation is a real goal. As Terry Eagleton points out, it "is not just that women should have equality of power and status with men; it is a questioning of all such power and status. It is not that the world will be better off with more female participation in it; it is that without the 'feminization' of human history, the world is unlikely to survive."

Publishing Fantasy Literature

David G. Hartwell

David G. Hartwell is a consulting editor for various publishers of fantasy literature. He explains how until Tolkien's *Lord of the Rings* proved the genre had staying power, fantasy books for adults were not taken very seriously by publishers. Then in the 1970s, Ballantine created Del Rey, a new imprint which would only publish fantasy. A flood of new books were written, leading other publishers to follow suit.

Fantasy fiction has been a significant part of literature since the early Gothic novels (such as Horace Walpole's *Castle of Otranto* and William Beckford's *Vathek*) and Jonathan Swift's *Gulliver's Travels*; as the form was developing, the earliest short stories were often fantasy stories. Indeed, tales of wonder and the fantastic are integral to all world literatures, are as old as recorded human imaginative thought. But as far as most serious readers today are concerned, ever since the mid-19th century, when Victorian culture demoted it to children's stories, fantasy fiction in English is for kids. Famous works—from *Alice's Adventures in Wonderland* by Lewis Carroll through *The Book of the Three Dragons* by Kenneth Morris to *A Wizard of Earthsea* by Ursula K. Le Guin—have tended to emerge from children's or young adult publishing.

FANTASY WAS NOT TAKEN SERIOUSLY

Fantasy for adults has been a rare, unusual and in large part unfashionable pleasure for nearly a century. I recall that when I was assigned E.M. Forster's *Aspects of the Novel* at Williams College, the chapter on fantasy was skipped. Later I read it and was introduced to such delights as *Flecker's*

Reprinted from "Dollars and Dragons: The Truth About Fantasy," by David G. Hartwell, *The New York Times Book Review*, April 29, 1990. Copyright © 1990 by David G. Hartwell. Reprinted by permission of the author and his agent, Susan Ann Protter.

Magic by Norman Matson. The whole modernist movement in literature rejected fantasy and dominated literary fashion to the extent that, for instance, James Branch Cabell's whole body of ornate mandarin fiction is nearly lost from sight, no more seriously considered than *Tarzan of the Apes,* though both were once read by adults for at least a generation.

So unfashionable did fantastic works become that fantasy was taken in during the 1930's and 40's under the umbrella of the growing antimodernist science fiction field, in such magazines as *Unknown, Fantastic Adventures* and *The Magazine of Fantasy & Science Fiction.* The latter is still very much a living magazine, though the era of commercial fiction magazines is long gone. Still, the notion that literate adults might read fantasy for pleasure did not take hold again until recently and is still a dubious proposition for most readers, given the amount of obvious silliness, junk and fiction for the immature on the adult fantasy bookshelves.

TOLKIEN PROVES FANTASY HAS ADULT APPEAL

It all started, in terms of genre publishing, with J.R.R. Tolkien's *Lord of the Rings* trilogy. This unique masterpiece of contemporary literature, praised by W.H. Auden and many others in the 50's, became a cult classic and a mass-market best-seller by the 60's. Tolkien's sales paid the light bills for its publisher, Ballantine Books, for nearly a decade; being smart publishers, Ian and Betty Ballantine cast about looking for ways to repeat that phenomenon. It took years. First they tried reprinting in paper other uniquely individual and powerfully original works excluded from the modernist canon: Mervyn Peake's Gormenghast trilogy, E.R. Eddison's *Worm Ouroboros* and his Zimiamvian trilogy. Then, in the late 1960's, they founded the Ballantine Adult Fantasy series, reprinting a book a month from the past century, bringing into mass editions nearly all the fantasy stories and novels worth reading—from William Morris's gorgeous medievalism to Evangeline Walton's literate retellings of Welsh mythology, Clark Ashton Smith's poetic visions, George MacDonald's moral allegories and H.P. Lovecraft's magnificent darkness. And, of course, the novels of James Branch Cabell. However, to their consternation, only the *Conan the Barbarian* series from Lancer Books caught on, with those now-famous Frank Frazetta covers. Barbarian fantasy sold, and it was the conventional wisdom that it sold to teen-age readers, not to the Tolkien audience.

Adult fantasy didn't sell well enough in its classic forms for Ballantine to support it, and the series was discontinued after several years, leaving in print only a few contemporary monuments, such as Peter S. Beagle's lively and sentimental fantasy classic, *The Last Unicorn*. Yet Ballantine knew that some kind of breakthrough had been made, that there was a market out there of adults, as well as teen-agers, who read and were still reading Tolkien in the millions and who could be sold fantasy if the right way could be found. And then they found it.

Lester del Rey, a Ballantine consulting editor, found it in the form of a manuscript by Terry Brooks entitled *The Sword of Shannara*. He went to Ron Busch, then the publisher of Ballantine Books, and mapped out his strategy. They would take this slavish imitation of Tolkien by an unknown writer and create a best-seller using mass-marketing techniques, and so satisfy the hunger in the marketplace for more Tolkien. Mr. del Rey, an experienced pulp editor and writer (he had edited a fantasy magazine in the 50's), knew what he was about—and it worked, much to the amazement and admiration of all the other marketers in publishing.

THE DEL REY FORMULA

Shortly thereafter, the Del Rey fantasy imprint was founded, with its criteria set up by Lester del Rey. The books would be original novels set in invented worlds in which magic works. Each would have a male central character who triumphed over the forces of evil (usually associated with technical knowledge of some variety) by innate virtue, and with the help of a tutor or tutelary spirit. Mr. del Rey had codified a children's literature that could be sold as adult. It was nostalgic, conservative, pastoral and optimistic. One critic seeking an explanation for why an American audience would adopt and support such a body of fiction has remarked that it was essentially a revival of the form of the utopian novel of the old South, the plantation novel in which life is rich and good, the lower classes are happy in their place and sing a lot, and evil resides in the technological North. The plot is the Civil War run backward: the South wins. That pattern seems to fit a majority of recent fantasy works well.

The covers would be rich, detailed illustrations of a colorful scene. Since unknown writers could be used, the cover art and production were often more costly than the advance paid to the writer. Through this process Mr. del Rey discovered another unknown writer, Stephen R. Donaldson—whose mammoth series *The Chronicles of Thomas Covenant, the Unbeliever*, which focuses on an ordinary man with leprosy transported into a fantasy land where he is forced to be a hero, is a work of great psychological power. (Joanna Russ has published a delicious parody, *Dragons and Dimwits*, whose hero, Thomas, points out the conspicuous unrealistic absence of meals: "'By St. Marx, and St. Engels,' said Thomas, 'and by St. Common Sense, I declare that neither thou nor thy people eatest or drinkest in the least (for I have never seen them do it) but subsistest upon fancies and fooleries imagined out of thin air.'") The series made Mr. Donaldson an enormous best-seller, thus proving the repeatability of his experiment on the largest scale in publishing.

By the late 70's, the success of the Del Rey formula was so confirmed that many other publishers had begun to publish in imitation. Dragons and unicorns began to appear all over the mass-market racks, and packaging codes with the proper subliminal and overt signals developed. A whole new mass-market genre had been established. One can understand it best in comparison to the toy market's discovery that you can sell dolls to boys if you call them action figures and make them hypermasculine. Writers such as Piers Anthony, a moderately successful and respected science fiction author who switched to fantasy, and Anne McCaffrey, a science fiction writer whose novels of a world of dragons could be marketed as fantasy, became Del Rey best-sellers. Everyone wanted in. In the 80's, most mass-market publishers did get in. Trilogies were the order of the day. Some writers complained that publishers often requested revisions in the endings of their fantasy works so that a single novel, if popular, might be extended by two more volumes. Lou Aronica, a Bantam vice president responsible for his company's fantasy publishing program, was interviewed in *SF Eye* magazine on his program's long-term success in publishing some works of high quality and low sales. "One of the reasons I have been able to do it for longer," he said, "is that I've been a little bit more willing to sell out for my list. I've published books that I don't like editorially, that I understand will sell a lot of copies." The implications of that attitude are manifest on America's bookshelves.

In 1990, we as readers are the inheritors of this phenomenon. Unquestionably, it created an enormous wave of trash writing to fill the neurotic hungers of an established audience trained in the 70's and in the past decade to accept tiny nuances and gestures overlaying mediocrity and repetition as true originality. Mr. Aronica commented that negative remarks from readers and critics "are actually being echoed in the responses we've seen from the marketplace. A lot of epic fantasy doesn't sell nearly as well as it used to sell, probably because there aren't too many new avenues being taken in epic fantasy, and readers are saying, 'Hey, I've read this book already, in fact I've read this book about fourteen times.'" It is enough to make one distrust all multivolume category works and any book with a unicorn depicted on the cover.

FANTASY STRIVES FOR EXCELLENCE

Yet the fantasy tradition in literature remains, at its peaks, a distinguished one. The Latin American school of magic realism, surely a literature for mature readers and widely influential in translation, is beyond the scope of this survey, but it should be noted that the editor of the respected Avon Books Latin American reprint program is also Avon's fantasy editor, John Douglas. Authentic works of the literary imagination have emerged in recent decades and should not be ignored by association with humble (category publishing) origins.

The various kinds of fashionable fiction in America have progressively, since the 30's, become obsessed with technique and with the nuances and gestures of ordinary characters in ordinary situations. They have exhausted in particular every avenue imaginable in illuminating the inner life of characters. Fantasy, on the other hand, manifests and dramatizes internal and psychological states, images and struggles as external and concrete, and focuses on the external actions of its characters. Fantasy fiction takes the reader clearly out of the world of reality. Sometimes the story begins in the "real" world, but it quickly becomes evident that behind the veil of real things and people another world exists, rich and strange and magical. The fantasy takes place in a world in which moral coordinates are clear and distinct, in a landscape in which moral qualities are most often embodied in major characters other than the central character (who is usually at first portrayed as an everyman, a fairly ordinary person of no particular consequence in the world).

But the central character becomes a crucial figure in a struggle between good and evil. This pattern has rich artistic possibilities when properly executed, especially when in the hands of the finest writers working in fantasy today.

There is a body of work, much of it published originally in paperback in the last two decades, which has not generally received adequate recognition for its literary excellence because of its origins in category publishing. Samuel R. Delany has written a four-volume series set in an imaginary world, Neveryon, that is a masterpiece of imagination and stylistic innovation. John Crowley's *Little, Big* is a dense, literate novel that is a standard against which others are now measured. Gene Wolfe's novels and stories, particularly the four-volume *Book of the New Sun,* are a significant contribution to American literature and the most important body of work in the fantasy field of the last decade.

And there are books by a number of younger writers: Ellen Kushner's *Swordspoint,* which challenges the moral assumptions of the category, and shuns magic, in prose that cuts like a blade; Orson Scott Card's multivolume *Tales of Alvin Maker,* which reimagines America according to Mormonism and retells the life of Joseph Smith, the religion's founder; Lisa Goldstein's *Red Magician,* which turns the hidden world of Eastern European Jews during the 1940's into a world of wonders, then transcends the Holocaust with a magical optimism; Terry Bisson's *Talking Man,* which tells of a cosmic battle that begins and ends in a junkyard in Kentucky.

And there are more: Paul Hazel's *Yearwood,* which breathes new life and intensity into a Celtic mythological world; Suzy McKee Charnas's cool, literate biography of a vampire in today's world, *The Vampire Tapestry;* Jonathan Carroll's slick novels of the contemporary world transformed by the fantastic, including *The Land of Laughs* and *Bones of the Moon,* and Guy Gavriel Kay's authentic reimagining of the Tolkienesque trilogy, *The Fionavar Tapestry.* All these works have individual excellences that are expanding the literary boundaries of stylistic and imaginative achievement in fantasy and in contemporary literature. . . .

While genre fantasy may still dominate the market, the fantastic in literature is healthy and growing in America. There are signs that the dominance of the genre by the best-selling, intensively marketed book, while it prevails, does provide a publishing home and a supportive audience for writers and for works of quality otherwise unsupported by fashion. As a mass-market phenomenon, the fantasy field can perhaps be understood as protectively covering a small body of work that is experimenting successfully with unfashionable techniques and subject matter rejected by the general literary culture in our time. And it seems a bad time for serious adult readers to reject, wholesale, the tale of wonder and the illumination of the human condition that fantasy has brought us throughout history.

Fantasy and Censorship

Michael O. Tunnel

Michael O. Tunnel, an associate professor at Brigham Young University and author of several children's books, fears there is no end in sight to censorship. For the past few decades more and more school systems and public libraries have been declaring fantasy books to be a bad influence. The usual argument is that the books are violent, frightening, and can cause children to lose touch with reality. Tunnel disputes these points and believes that if censorship continues, it will be young readers who lose in the long run.

> About once every hundred years some wiseacre gets up and tries to banish the fairy tale. Perhaps I had better say a few words in its defence, as reading for children.
>
> —C.S. Lewis

C.S. Lewis was compelled to write his defense of fantasy stories, particularly traditional tales, in 1952. Yet, in far less than a hundred years, "wiseacres" are trying to banish not only the fairy tale but also much of modern fantasy literature for children. We seem to have entered a new age of censorship, as reflected by the American Library Association's ever-growing annual list of censorship cases affecting schools and public libraries. Within the last decade, both the National Council of Teachers of English and the International Reading Association have joined the American Library Association in its acute concern about the forces that want to restrict our children's intellectual freedom.

According to children's book editor Phyllis J. Fogleman, censorship letters received by publishers in the 1970s and 80s mostly complained about sexuality, "but now censors are broadening their scope to include anything that seems even vaguely anti-Christian to them. For a number of fundamentalist groups, certain words are seen as red flags. If a book simply includes the words *devil* and *witch*, it's enough

Excerpted from "The Double-Edged Sword: Fantasy and Censorship," by Michael O. Tunnel, *Language Arts*, vol. 71, December 1994, pp. 606–11. Copyright © 1994 by the National Council of Teachers of English. Reprinted with permission.

to cause these people to file a complaint." She points out that even *The Wizard of Oz* was attacked in Tennessee for portraying witches in too positive a fashion.

Following in the footsteps of C.S. Lewis, I also would like to defend the fairy tale and its other fantasy relatives. Instead of a genre that threatens our children, fantasy is fundamentally the most important kind of story to share with them. I can best support this premise by offering an answer—perhaps a challenge—to each of the major objections to fantasy stories. Though there are a variety of complaints, most seem to fall into four categories.

LOSING TOUCH WITH REALITY

There are adults who fear that fairy tales and fantasy will lead children to be somehow out of touch with reality, that they will be less likely to distinguish fact from fancy if they are read too many fairy stories. "Do fairy tales teach children to retreat into a world of wish-fulfillment—'fantasy' in the technical psychological sense of the word—instead of facing the problems of the real world?" asks C.S. Lewis. Of course not, he concludes, and goes on to say that realistic "school stories" written for young readers are far more likely to cause problems.

> I do not mean that school stories for boys and girls ought not to be written. I am only saying that they are far more liable to become "fantasies" in the clinical sense than fantastic stories are. And this distinction holds for adult reading too. The dangerous fantasy is always superficially realistic. The real victim of wishful reverie does not batten on *The Odyssey, The Tempest,* or *The Worm of Ouroboros:* he [or she] prefers stories about millionaires, irresistible beauties, posh hotels, palm beaches, and bedroom scenes—things that really might happen, that ought to happen, that would have happened if the reader had had a fair chance. For, as I say, there are two kinds of longing. The one is an *askesis,* a spiritual exercise, and the other is a disease.

In fact, according to eminent child psychologist Bruno Bettleheim, children deprived of a rich fantasy life are more likely to search for a magical means of coping with the realities of daily living:

> Many young people who today suddenly seek escape in drug-induced dreams, apprentice themselves to some guru, believe in astrology, engage in practicing "black magic," or who in some other fashion escape from reality into daydreams about

magic experiences which are to change their life for the better, were prematurely pressed to view reality in an adult way.

Fairy tales and fantasy are prescriptions for mental health, not disease-causing agents. "Myth making is essential in gaining mental health, and the compassionate therapist will not discourage it," says Rollo May, the world-renowned psychiatrist. "Indeed, the very birth and proliferation of psychotherapy in our contemporary age were called forth by the disintegration of our myths." Children denied the opportunity to dream of magical lands and imaginary solutions to terrible problems may be less capable as teenagers and adults of coping with harsh or troubling realities.

For example, coping devices may act like the safety valve on the boiler of a steam engine and have helped many a child (and adult) deal with stress. A small child, for instance, is completely controlled by an adult world—told when to eat, when to sleep, what to wear. But in fairy tales, it is often the youngest son or daughter or the weak, seemingly less able character, rather than parents or other power figures, who wins the day: Hansel and Gretel, Cinderella, or the youngest son in Grimm's "The Water of Life." Children vicariously vent frustrations in healthy ways by subconsciously identifying with such heroes. They also are given a sense of hope about their ultimate abilities to succeed in the world. Maurice Sendak's *Where the Wild Things Are* (1963) mirrors just such a process occurring in the life of a child. Max, banished to his room without any supper, is filled with rage and is helpless to change his lot. He channels his anger and frustration into a wild fantasy, in which he travels "to where the wild things are." All powerful, Max tames the terrible beasts and becomes "king of all wild things" until his anger is properly vented, and then he misses the good things about home. Sendak creates a marvelous story in the fairy tale tradition and at the same time reveals a bit of truth about the positive attributes of fantasies. Of course, *Where the Wild Things Are* has been challenged by censors and nervous parents since its publication, partly because the idea of a child defying parental authority by escaping into a dream world seems unhealthy—a negative message to children.

Censors worried about anti-Christian issues in stories also are troubled by the psychological aspects of fantasy. They seem to worry that the escapism of fantasy leads children into the occult or Satanism. Of all the books (adult and children's titles cutting across all genres) reported as challenged or banned by the *Newsletter on Intellectual Freedom* during a period from March 1992 to March 1993, 20% were fantasies for which the complaints included the words *anti-Christian, occult, Satanism,* or *witchcraft.* Take, for example, Zilpha Keatley Snyder's Newbery Honor Book, *The Headless Cupid* (1971). It is the story of an unhappy step-sibling who awes and frightens her new brothers and sisters by pretending to have mystical powers. Though she is a complete fraud, a few unexplainable ghostly events nevertheless do occur. In 1989 at the Hays (Kansas) Public Library, *The Headless Cupid* was challenged "because it [*The Headless Cupid*] could lead young readers to embrace Satanism." Again, in 1992, complaints surfaced in the Escondido, California, school system "because it [*The Headless Cupid*] contains references to the occult."

VIOLENCE IN FANTASY

Just as a cry has gone up from many societal watchdogs about violence on television, film, and even in pop music, censors have long protested the violence in many traditional tales. Modern high fantasy stories, the type of fantasy most like fairy tales (such as Tolkien's *Lord of the Rings* trilogy or Alexander's *Prydain Chronicles*), have suffered similar criticism. Critics suggest that the so-called violent acts in these stories will breed violence in children. However, this supposition is refuted by the work of Ephraim Biblow. Biblow explains the results of an experimental study which revealed that children with rich fantasy lives (which fairy stories stimulate) who were exposed to a film with aggressive content responded to the experience with a significant decrease in aggressive behavior. "Low-fantasy" children showed no decrease but a tendency toward increased aggression. Furthermore, Biblow's study clearly indicated that children skilled in "fantasy usage," who therefore engage in aggressive fantasies, are less aggressive during play activities and times of confrontation. Note the concluding sentences of Biblow's report:

> The low-fantasy child, as observed during play, presented himself as more motorically oriented, revealed much action and little thought in play activities. The high-fantasy child in contrast was more highly structured and creative and tended to be verbally rather than physically aggressive.

Contrary to a popular belief, frequent trips into the land of faerie make for creative thinkers and problem solvers who are less physically aggressive—certainly qualities most parents desire for their children. For instance, many of us remember using "white knight" fantasies to defuse our hostilities, and these fantasies were often patterned on fairy stories. For example, a bully terrorizes you. You are helpless. In your fantasy, you must protect someone more helpless than yourself, but now you have the power to take control. After giving the bully sufficient warning, you soundly thrash him. I, for one, always felt better after this type of daydream and was less apt to vent my anger on innocent victims like siblings or friends.

Still, some detractors may say that the above reasons are not enough to warrant the violence. Perhaps they need to understand the archetypal nature of traditional stories and their modern counterparts, in which characters often represent or symbolize basic human character traits. The padding is pulled away in these stories, and we are allowed to examine the rudiments of human behavior, painted for us in primary colors. The old stories have existed for centuries mainly because they speak to us on a deep level concerning the human experience. Because good and evil are the most basic of human traits, children are concerned from an early age with the ramifications of good and bad behavior. In classic fantasy stories, there are few gradations of good and bad—the evil characters are truly evil and cannot be swayed toward good. Likewise, the pure in heart remain pure. These stories, then, are a study in justice, or, as Huck, Hepler, and Hickman put it: "Poetic justice prevails; the good and the just are eventually rewarded, while the evil are punished. This appeals to the child's sense of justice and his moral judgment."

Kohlberg's stages of moral development describe the young child as being in the "Premoral Stage" (up to about 8 years), which basically means that "the child believes that evil behavior is likely to be punished, and good behavior is based on obedience or the avoidance of evil implicit in disobedience." According to Bettleheim, the evil person meeting a well-deserved fate in the fairy tale satisfies a child's deep need for justice to prevail. Sometimes this means destroying the evil altogether. Author and literary critic G.K. Chesterton told the story of some children with whom he saw Maeterlinck's play *The Blue Bird*. They were unhappy because there was no "Day of Judgment" for the wicked character. His clear understanding of children's moral development elicited this deeply meaningful response from Chesterton: "For children are innocent and love justice; while most of us are wicked and naturally prefer mercy." A study conducted with first-grade students supports Chesterton's observation. When asked to choose a preferred ending to "Little Red Riding Hood" from three variations of the tale, the children selected the ending in which the wolf was made to suffer the most. The children demanded that the villain pay dearly for his crimes.

I think it is important to examine exactly what elements are labeled as violent in fairy tales and in quality works of modern fantasy. Take one of the bloodier fairy tales, Grimm's version of "Cinderella," for example. Both truly wicked stepsisters mutilate themselves (trimming heel and cutting off toe) so that the slipper might fit. Only the blood reveals their treachery. Later, the birds peck out their eyes. Yet, the tale very simply and compactly describes each violent act. We don't read of viscous fluid streaming down faces or blood spurting on walls and floors. That's the stuff of slasher horror movies, sensationalism designed to titillate, not a careful comment on justice.

The better works of modern high fantasy handle violence in the same manner. In the final book of Lloyd Alexander's Prydain series, the arch villain Arawn Death-Lord is confronted for the first time. He shape-shifts into the form of a serpent, but nevertheless is destroyed. Note the controlled images Alexander gives of Arawn's violent death.

> Taran swung the flashing sword with all his strength. The blade clove the serpent in two. . . .

> A horrified gasp came from Eilonwy. Taran looked up as the girl pointed to the cloven serpent. Its body writhed, its shape blurred. In its place appeared the black-cloaked figure of a man whose severed head had rolled face downward on the earth. Yet in a moment this shape too lost its form and the corpse sank like a shadow into the earth; and where it had lain was seared and fallow, the ground wasted, fissured as though by drought. Arawn Death-Lord had vanished.

Violence in stories also appears to compound the complaints of those who see fantasy as anti-Christian. C.S. Lewis's immortal classic, *The Lion, the Witch and the Wardrobe* (1950), was challenged in 1990 in the Howard County, Maryland, Public Schools because of "graphic violence, mysticism and gore." The sacrifice of the great lion, Aslan, who represents Christ in this Christian allegory, is probably the most violent and gory scene, evoking images of the crucifixion from the New Testament. But the charge of "mysticism" combined with that of "graphic violence" relegates Lewis's allegory to the realm of the occult.

FRIGHTENING FOR YOUNG CHILDREN

Related to violence is the fright factor of fantasy stories, particularly the fairy tales. For instance, many parents worry that the original Grimm's version of "Snow White" or "Cinderella" will cause their young children to have nightmares or other sorts of distress. However, dangerous story elements in fairy tales, such as wicked witches or dragons, are far removed in both time and place from the lives of children; therefore these tales prove much less frightening than realistic stories of danger that focus on real-life fears. Well-meaning parents often program children to be afraid by telegraphing their anxiety when they assume elements of a story will cause alarm. The truth is that we are unable to predict what will frighten a child in this manner. I was mystified by some of my children being afraid of the dark and others not. Nevertheless, we as parents wish to insulate our children from fear. Yet to completely insulate them may be a disservice, as C.S. Lewis points out.

> Those who say that children must not be frightened may mean two things. They may mean (1) that we must not do anything likely to give the child those haunting, disabling, pathological fears against which ordinary courage is helpless: in fact, *phobias*. . . . Or they may mean (2) that we must try to keep out of his mind the knowledge that he is born into a world of death, violence, wounds, adventure, heroism and cowardice, good and evil. If they mean the first I agree. . . . [However] the second would indeed be to give children a false impression and feed them on escapism in the bad sense. . . . Since it is so likely they will meet cruel enemies, let them at least have heard of brave knights and heroic courage. Otherwise you are making their destiny not bright but darker. . . . Nothing will persuade me that [a fairy tale] causes an ordinary child any kind or degree of fear beyond what it wants, and needs, to feel. For, of course, it wants to be a little frightened.

An ironic outcome of trying to protect children from fairy tales is that parents may indeed be frightening them instead! Ann Trousdale tells the story of a friend who only read softened versions of the fairy and folktales to her young daughter. The rendering of "The Three Little Pigs" that she chose eliminated the violent elements found in the original Joseph Jacobs version: The first two pigs were not eaten; the wolf was not boiled alive. Instead, the wolf came down the chimney, burned his derriere, rocketed back up the chimney, and ran off into the distance, never to been seen again. The little girl said, "He's gonna come back," and began to have nightmares. Trousdale provided a copy of the original version and soon received a letter that said, "Well, we put the Big Bad Wolf to rest." Perhaps this is another example of a child's need for justice to prevail, but it seems even more basic: The evil was destroyed, and thus the threat was eliminated.

What fairy tales provide children is a message of hope, not fear. As Joseph Campbell suggests, a child who follows "a multitude of heroic figures through the classic stages of the universal adventure" will come to understand "the singleness of the human spirit in its aspirations, powers, vicissitudes, and wisdom." Indeed, no matter how dark the path or how bleak the outlook, fairy tales declare that we have an excellent chance of making it through and coming out on top. The happy ending is an essential part of fairy stories.

Jim Trelease believes that fairy tales simply confirm what children already know or, at least, suspect about the world: It's often a cruel and dangerous place. But fairy tales take children far beyond this grim reality, calling upon their sense of courage and adventure and advising: "Take your courage in hand and go out to meet that world head on." In fact, children who recoil from strong images of danger in fairy tales have the most to gain from the exposure.

Fantasy stories targeted by censors as frightening are typically written for younger children, who are deemed to be more easily alarmed. Fairy tales and ghost stories appear frequently on lists of challenged books for young readers. For example, Alvin Schwartz's popular ghost tales, *Scary Stories to Tell in the Dark* (1981), has been challenged repeatedly since its publication. In 1992, challenges were mounted in school districts in Arizona, Connecticut, Indiana, and Washington. Even scary poetry for children has been attacked. Jack Prelutsky's *The Headless Horseman Rides Tonight and Other Poems to Trouble Your Sleep* (1980) was challenged in 1982 at the Victor Elementary School in Rochester, New York, because it "was too frightening for young children to read." Over the years I have asked my graduate students, who are practicing primary- and intermediate-grade teachers, if Prelutsky's poems have frightened their students. Never have I been told "yes."

Chronology

1812

Jacob and Wilhelm Grimm's *Fairy Tales:* A much-valued collection of tales that continue to inspire writers today.

1846

Hans Christian Andersen's *Fairy Tales:* Seemingly timeless tales, many of these stories have been adapted and retold in a number of different versions over the last century.

1856

William Morris's "The Hollow Land," "Golden Wings," and other stories appear in *Oxford and Cambridge Magazine:* Author of a number of surreal short stories (and later novels), he is considered by purists to be the father of "modern fantasy."

1858

George MacDonald's *Phantastes: A Faerie Romance for Men and Women:* A theologian, his book represented the first published full-length fantasy novel.

1865

Lewis Carroll's *Alice's Adventures in Wonderland:* one of the best-known early works of popular fantasy.

1871

George MacDonald's *At the Back of the North Wind:* Initially a children's novel, this work was appreciated by adults as well.

1882

Carlo Collodi's *Pinocchio:* Another children's story that found a market with adults, this book was the basis of the famous Disney film that was created about sixty years later.

1886

William Morris's *A Dream of John Ball:* Though Morris had gained notoriety as a writer of short stories, this was his first full-length novel.

1900

L. Frank Baum's *The Wonderful Wizard of Oz:* the first book in a series that gained popular success at the turn of the century; it is best known as the basis for one of Hollywood's most endearing classic films.

1904

James Barrie's *Peter Pan:* Another children's story, this tale gained an enormous following with adults as it was recreated over the last century through animated features, live-action movies, theme-park rides, and Broadway shows.

1922

A.A. Milne's *Winnie-the-Pooh:* the classic tale of the inhabitants of the Hundred-Acre Woods; Milne's stories have been kept alive over nearly a century, in part due to its Disney mainstreaming.

1923

Weird Tales: a pulp magazine of fantasy and science fiction.

1937

J.R.R. Tolkien's *The Hobbit:* the precursor to Tolkien's famous trilogy.

1938

T.H. White's *The Sword in the Stone:* the popular and painstakingly researched retelling of the Arthurian legend.

1945

George Orwell's *Animal Farm:* Typically a science-fiction writer, Orwell created this surreal story as a vehicle for discussing social and political philosophy.

1950

C.S. Lewis's *The Lion, the Witch, and the Wardrobe:* the first book in the *Chronicles of Narnia,* a collection that combined Lewis's religious outlook and interest in fantasy.

1954–1955

J.R.R. Tolkien's *The Lord of the Rings:* One of the most compelling and important works of modern fantasy, these books launched a kind of popular success in the literary industry that is still being felt today.

1968

Ursula K. Le Guin's *A Wizard of Earthsea:* This work of high fantasy represented one of the first commercial successes in the genre for a female author.

1968

Anne McCaffrey's *Dragonflight:* the first book in the Dragon Riders of Pern series, one of the largest popular successes of the genre in the 1970s and 1980s.

1970

Roger Zelazny's *Nine Princes in Amber:* the first book in the Amber series.

1977

Piers Anthony's *A Spell for Chameleon:* the first book in the Xanth series, marking the beginning of one of fantasy's most prolific careers; Steven R. Donaldson's *Chronicles of Thomas Covenant the Unbeliever:* based on the adventures of a man who struggles with leprosy while fulfilling his overwhelming and unwanted destiny.

1990

Robert Jordan's *Eye of the World:* The first book in the Wheel of Time series, which would span more than a decade and achieve a commercial success and dedicated fan base similar to Tolkien's.

1998

J.K. Rowling's Harry Potter series begins with *Harry Potter and the Sorcerer's Stone:* This series represents one of the highest-grossing book sales in the history of literature; the release in 2000 of the fourth book, *Harry Potter and the Goblet of Fire,* was met with an anticipation that made international headlines.

FOR FURTHER RESEARCH

BOOKS

Brian Attebery, *The Fantasy Tradition in American Literature: From Irving to Le Guin*. Bloomington: Indiana University Press, 1980.

Robert H. Boyer and Kenneth J. Zahorski, eds., *Fantasists on Fantasy: A Collection of Critical Reflections by Eighteen Masters of the Art*. New York: Avon Books, 1984.

Sheila Egoff, ed., *Only Connect: Readings on Children's Literature*. 3rd ed. Ontario: Oxford University Press, 1996.

Ralph Waldo Emerson, "Experience," in *Essays: Second Series*. Philadelphia: David McKay, 1888.

Kath Filmer-Davies, *Scepticism and Hope in Twentieth Century Fantasy Literature*. Bowling Green, OH: Bowling Green State University Popular Press, 1992.

Northrop Frye, *Fables of Identity: Studies in Poetic Mythology*. New York: Harbinger Books, 1963.

Rosemary Jackson, *Fantasy: The Literature of Subversion*. New York: Methuen, 1981.

Ursula K. Le Guin, *The Language of the Night: Essays on Fantasy and Science Fiction*. New York: HarperCollins, 1992.

C.S. Lewis, "On Three Ways of Writing for Children," in *Of Other Worlds: Essays and Stories*. Ed. Walter Hooper. New York: Harcourt, Brace, and World, 1965.

T.E. Little, *The Fantasts: Studies in J.R.R. Tolkien, Lewis Carroll, Mervyn Peake, Nikolay Gogol, and Kenneth Grahame*. Amersham, England: Avebury, 1984.

Richard Matthews, *Fantasy: The Liberation of Imagination*. New York: Twayne, 1997.

Donald E. Morse, ed., *The Celebration of the Fantastic: Se-lected Papers from the Tenth Anniversary International Conference on the Fantastic in the Arts.* Westport, CT: Greenwood, 1992.

Glenn Edward Sadler, ed., *Teaching Children's Literature: Is-sues, Pedagogy, Resources.* New York: Modern Language Association of America, 1992.

Joe Sanders, *Functions of the Fantastic: Selected Essays from the Thirteenth International Conference on the Fantastic in the Arts.* Westport, CT: Greenwood, 1995.

Roger C. Schlobin, ed., *The Aesthetics of Fantasy Literature and Art.* Notre Dame, IN: University of Notre Dame Press, 1982.

Charlotte Spivack, *Merlin's Daughters.* Westport, CT: Green-wood, 1987.

Ann Swinfen, *In Defence of Fantasy: A Study of the Genre in English and American Literature Since 1945.* London and Boston: Routledge & Kegan Paul, 1984.

John H. Timmerman, *Other Worlds: The Fantasy Genre.* Bowling Green, OH: Bowling Green State University Popular Press, 1983.

Lois Parkinson Zamora and Wendy B. Faris, eds., *Magical Realism: Theory, History, Community.* Durham, NC: Duke University Press, 1995.

PERIODICALS

Mairi Brahim and Sue Cullinan, "Person of the Year 2000/Runners-Up: The Magic of Potter: J.K. Rowling's Wiz-ardry Turned On a New Generation to That Old Tech-nology, the Wondrous Printed Word," *Time*, December 12, 2000.

Carolyn Caywood, "The Quest for Character," *School Library Journal*, vol. 41, no. 3, March 1995.

Susan Dexter, "Tricks of the Wizard's Trade," *Writer*, vol. 110, no. 11, November 1997.

David G. Hartwell, "Dollars and Dragons: The Truth About Fantasy," *New York Times Book Review*, April 29, 1990.

Malcolm Jones, "Why Harry's Hot," *Newsweek*, July 17, 2000.

Susan Lehr, "Fantasy: Inner Journeys for Today's Child," *Publishing Research Quarterly*, Fall 1991.

C.S. Lewis, "The Gods Return to Earth," *Time and Tide*, August 15, 1954.

C.N. Manlove, "Comic Fantasy," *Extrapolation*, vol. 28, no. 1, 1987.

Tamora Pierce, "Fantasy: Why Kids Read It, Why Kids Need It," *School Library Journal*, vol. 39, no. 10, October 1993.

Terry Pratchett, "Imaginary Worlds, Real Stories," *Folklore*, vol. 111, 2000.

William Provost, "Language and Myth in the Fantasy Writings of J.R.R. Tolkien," *Modern Age: A Quarterly Review*, vol. 33, no. 1, Spring 1990.

Edward Rothstein, "An Adored Fantasy Series Now Hints at 1990s' Angst," *The New York Times*, October 26, 1998.

———, "Flaming Swords and Wizard's Orbs," *New York Times Book Review*, December 8, 1996.

Dwayne Thorpe, "Fantasy Characterization: The Example of Tolkien," *Mythlore*, no. 66, Summer 1991.

Michael O. Tunnel, "The Double-Edged Sword: Fantasy and Censorship," *Language Arts*, vol. 71, December 1994.

INDEX